SEND
STRATEGIES FOR THE SECONDARY YEARS

OTHER TITLES FROM BLOOMSBURY EDUCATION

100 Ideas for Secondary Teachers: Supporting Students with ADHD by Jannine Perryman

100 Ideas for Secondary Teachers: Supporting Students with Dyslexia by Gavin Reid and Shannon Green

100 Ideas for Secondary Teachers: Supporting Students with Numeracy Difficulties by Patricia Babtie and Sue Dillon

Creating Belonging in the Classroom: A practical guide to having brave and difficult conversations by Zahara Chowdhury

The Inclusive Classroom: A new approach to differentiation by Daniel Sobel and Sara Alston

The Ultimate Guide to Adaptive Teaching: Confidently meeting the needs of every learner by Sue Cowley

SEND

STRATEGIES FOR THE SECONDARY YEARS

Practical ideas and expert advice to support and understand young people

GEORGINA DURRANT

BLOOMSBURY EDUCATION
LONDON OXFORD NEW YORK NEW DELHI SYDNEY

BLOOMSBURY EDUCATION
Bloomsbury Publishing Plc
50 Bedford Square, London, WC1B 3DP, UK
Bloomsbury Publishing Ireland Limited
29 Earlsfort Terrace, Dublin 2, Ireland

BLOOMSBURY, BLOOMSBURY EDUCATION and the Diana logo are trademarks of
Bloomsbury Publishing Plc

This edition published in Great Britain, 2026 by Bloomsbury Publishing Plc

Text copyright © Georgina Durrant, 2026

Georgina Durrant has asserted her right under the Copyright, Designs and Patents Act,
1988, to be identified as Author of this work

All contributions are copyright of the contributor named.

Bloomsbury Publishing Plc does not have any control over, or responsibility for, any
third-party websites referred to or in this book. All internet addresses given in this
book were correct at the time of going to press. The author and publisher regret any
inconvenience caused if addresses have changed or sites have ceased to exist, but
can accept no responsibility for any such changes

All rights reserved. No part of this publication may be: i) reproduced or
transmitted in any form, electronic or mechanical, including photocopying, recording
or by means of any information storage or retrieval system without prior permission
in writing from the publishers; or ii) used or reproduced in any way for the training,
development or operation of artificial intelligence (AI) technologies, including
generative AI technologies. The rights holders expressly reserve this publication
from the text and data mining exception as per Article 4(3) of the
Digital Single Market Directive (EU) 2019/790

A catalogue record for this book is available from the British Library

ISBN: PB: 978-1-80199-714-0; ePub: 978-1-80199-712-6

2 4 6 8 10 9 7 5 3 1 (paperback)

Text design by Marcus Duck

Typeset by Lumina Datamatics Ltd
Printed and bound in Great Britain by TJ Books, Padstow, Cornwall

To find out more about our authors and books visit www.bloomsbury.com
and sign up for our newsletters

For product safety related questions contact productsafety@bloomsbury.com

DEDICATION

I dedicate this book to every teenager with SEND whose needs have gone unmet. May this book, in some small way, help to bring about understanding and the support you deserve.

ACKNOWLEDGEMENTS

I would like to thank Bloomsbury and, in particular, my wonderful editor Emily Evans. Thank you for your support and for inviting me to write another book!

Thank you to everyone who shared such positive reviews of this book's predecessor *SEND Strategies for the Primary Years*: the lovely comments, photos and reviews really motivated me to write this follow-up book.

A huge thank you to everyone who helped to inform this book. I am so grateful to the many people who provided me with their time, guidance, advice and expertise. Thank you to the families and teachers who spoke to me so openly about their difficult experiences with the current SEND system. And a special thank you to the young people and adults with lived experience of SEND, who shared their advice and experiences in the introductions of each chapter. I think you'll agree that the case studies bring this book to life and remind us of our purpose.

Thank you to my family: my wonderful husband, absolutely amazing children and my brilliant mum, dad and brother. My mum has once again diligently read through the draft copies of this book for me. Don't tell her, but I couldn't do this without her!

CONTENTS

VIII
INTRODUCTION

1
CHAPTER 1:
SPEECH, LANGUAGE AND COMMUNICATION SKILLS

29
CHAPTER 2:
LITERACY SKILLS

49
CHAPTER 3:
NUMERACY SKILLS

63
CHAPTER 4:
MOTOR SKILLS

86
CHAPTER 5:
SENSORY PROCESSING DIFFERENCES

112
CHAPTER 6:
EMOTIONAL REGULATION

129
CHAPTER 7:
CONCENTRATION AND ORGANISATION SKILLS

150
REFERENCES

157
INDEX

INTRODUCTION

Postcode Lottery. Broken. Crisis. Underresourced. Inequitable. These are just some of the words dominating headlines when discussing the current state of the SEND system, a system meant to support children and young people with Special Educational Needs and Disabilities (SEND). Even our Education Secretary, Bridget Phillipson, has described it as 'neglected to the point of crisis' (TES, 2024a).

I could delve into the details: the rising number of children and young people with SEND, now reaching 1.6 million, an increase of 6.4 per cent in just one year (DfE, 2025); the ridiculously long waiting times for assessments and external support; the hurdles around Education Health Care Plans (EHCPs). But let's be honest, that's not why you're here. You didn't pick up this book to dwell on the challenges. You're here because you want solutions.

While I'd love to influence and improve the SEND system to better serve the children and young people who need it (a hopeful wave to the Department for Education here!), this book isn't about waiting for change that may take years. It's about the present, the children and young people sitting in classrooms today who need support *now*. They cannot afford to wait for a system overhaul.

I've written this book (and its predecessor *SEND Strategies for the Primary Years*) to equip you – teachers, parents, carers – with practical strategies, insights and resources that you can use to make a real difference in the lives of young people with SEND. It's not just about fixing the system; it's about supporting the children who cannot wait for it to be fixed.

LIMITATIONS OF THE BOOK

As educators, parents and carers, we must remember that diagnosing a child with specific SEND is not something we can do, nor should we make assumptions about potential diagnoses. With this in mind, I've intentionally structured this book around areas of need rather than a specific SEND diagnosis, ensuring the focus remains on practical solutions that benefit all children.

If you're a parent and you suspect your child may have specific SEND, the first step is often to speak to the school's Special Educational Needs and Disabilities Coordinator (SENDCo). They have established processes for gathering insights into a young person's needs, including discussions with teachers, the young person and their family, as well as observations during lessons. Based on this, the SENDCo may seek advice or refer the young person for assessments conducted by external professionals.

Although we cannot provide diagnoses ourselves, there is so much we can do to support children with SEND while they wait. For example, if a young person is finding it difficult to concentrate in lessons and may later be diagnosed with Attention Deficit Hyperactivity Disorder (ADHD), you don't have to wait for that diagnosis to help them manage their focus more effectively. Whether it's introducing movement breaks, adjusting seating arrangements, or offering strategies to maintain engagement, these interventions can be game-changing for the young person. Similarly, a young person who finds spelling particularly challenging may go on to receive a diagnosis of dyslexia, or perhaps not, but while they wait, we can still provide tools and techniques to ease their struggles.

This book is designed for precisely this purpose: to address the common areas of need for young people with SEND or those who may have SEND, and to offer practical strategies that you can implement immediately. Whether in the classroom or at home, these approaches aim to make a meaningful difference for the young people in your care, starting today.

HOW TO USE THIS BOOK

I have divided this book into seven chapters, each for a specific area of need, designed for you to dip in and out of as and when:

1. Speech, language and communication skills
2. Literacy skills
3. Numeracy skills
4. Motor skills
5. Sensory processing differences
6. Emotional regulation
7. Concentration and organisation skills.

Each chapter follows a consistent structure:

- **CASE STUDIES:** Each chapter opens with reflections from young people and adults who have firsthand experience with neurodivergence or SEND. They share the challenges they faced during their secondary school years, what strategies helped and what didn't.

- ▶ **OVERVIEW OF NEEDS:** I explain what these areas of need mean, the wider impact on the young person if these specific needs aren't supported, as well as which specific SEND may make some young people find these skills inherently more difficult.

- ▶ **WHAT YOU MIGHT NOTICE:** While we can't and must not attempt to diagnose a young person ourselves, I explain how you may notice those who perhaps don't have a specific diagnosis (or are waiting) but may have difficulties in these areas. For instance, a young person with Speech, Language, and Communication Needs (SLCN) might appear withdrawn or frustrated during lessons.

- ▶ **STRATEGIES:** You'll find a range of practical strategies, adjustments and ideas to help support young people both at school and at home. As these strategies may vary depending on if you're supporting children in the classroom, across the school as a SENDCo and/or school leader or as a family member at home, I've split these into the different settings.

- ▶ **RESOURCES:** I've included a curated selection of resources to help support young people in developing the particular skills addressed in each chapter.

- ▶ **FURTHER READING AND SUPPORT:** At the end of each chapter, I suggest additional books, websites and tools to expand your understanding.

I want to emphasise that every strategy in this book is grounded in a neuro-affirming approach. By this, I mean we are not seeking to change neurodivergent young people or make them fit into neurotypical moulds. Instead, we focus on creating the right conditions for them to thrive and develop a strong, positive sense of identity.

This book is the result of conversations and consultations with a wide array of people, including young people with SEND, their families, SENDCos, teachers, teaching assistants, headteachers, Educational Psychologists (EPs), Occupational Therapists (OTs), Speech and Language Therapists (SaLTs), and many others. And I'm incredibly grateful for their time in helping inform this book.

Most of all, I owe enormous gratitude to the young people and adults who have shared their personal stories for the case studies featured in each chapter. You may notice a common pattern in the case studies: the wish that their needs had been recognised, understood and supported sooner. This recurring theme has been a powerful motivator for creating this book and its focus on the importance of timely identification and meaningful support.

ACRONYMS AND THEIR DEFINITIONS

- AAC – Augmentative and Alternative Communication
- ACE – Adverse Childhood Experience
- ADHD – Attention Deficit Hyperactivity Disorder
- ASC – Autism Spectrum Condition (formerly ASD – Autism Spectrum Disorder)
- BSL – British Sign Language
- CAMHS – Child and Adolescence Mental Health Services
- DCD – Developmental Coordination Disorder (also known as dyspraxia)
- DLD – Developmental Language Disorder (formerly SLI – Specific Language Impairment)
- EAL – English as an Additional Language
- EDS – Ehlers-Danlos Syndrome
- EHCNA – Education, Health Care Needs Assessment
- EHCP – Education, Health and Care Plan
- EP – Educational Psychologist
- FAS – Foetal Alcohol Syndrome
- FXS – Fragile X Syndrome
- GDD – Global Developmental Delay
- LA – Local Authority
- OT – Occupational Therapist
- PDA – Pathological Demand Avoidance
- SaLT – Speech and Language Therapist
- SLT – Senior Leadership Team
- SEMH – Social, Emotional and Mental Health
- SEND – Special Educational Needs and Disabilities
- SENDCo – Special Educational Needs and Disabilities Coordinator
- SLCN – Speech, Language and Communication Needs
- TA – Teaching Assistant

WHO AM I AND WHY HAVE I WRITTEN THIS BOOK?

My name is Georgina Durrant, and I've been fortunate enough to dedicate my career to supporting children and young people with SEND. I'm a former secondary teacher and SENDCo, the founder of a SEND tutoring service, creator of The SEN Resources Blog (a website designed to provide support to parents/carers and teachers of children with SEND) and the author of four, and soon to be five, published books on SEND.

I have the privilege of speaking at conferences and working with schools to share strategies for SEND support. I've also contributed to important policy discussions, including at a parliamentary round table and the Westminster Education Forum, which has been an incredible opportunity to advocate for improvements in SEND provision. Occasionally, you'll find me – on TV, radio or in the national press – 'banging the drum' (or... passionately raising awareness!) and sharing practical advice to improve provision and support for children and young people with SEND.

I host the SEND podcast, *SEND in the Experts with Georgina Durrant*. And through the podcast, I've had the absolute privilege of speaking with professionals and inspiring people with lived experience of SEND who share their expertise to help families, teachers and carers to better understand and support young people.

This book builds on all that work, continuing the journey I began with *SEND Strategies for the Primary Years*. It isn't about solving every systemic issue in the SEND world (if only we could!). Instead, it's about offering practical, realistic strategies that you can use to support the children and young people in your care right now. I'm incredibly grateful to everyone who has contributed their insights to this book, including young people with SEND, their families, teachers, SENDCos, therapists and other professionals. Their voices are at the heart of this book, and I hope it makes a difference to the young people you parent or teach.

CHAPTER 1
SPEECH, LANGUAGE AND COMMUNICATION SKILLS

CASE STUDY

MADISON, AGED 17, WRITES ABOUT HER EXPERIENCES WITH SPEECH, LANGUAGE AND COMMUNICATION NEEDS AS AN AUTISTIC STUDENT. SHE SHARES THE STRATEGIES THAT WERE USEFUL AND THOSE THAT WERE NOT SO HELPFUL WHILE AT SECONDARY SCHOOL.

Many people have speech, language and communication needs for many reasons. I am autistic and this is where my communication needs come from. Sometimes I can struggle to communicate how I am thinking and feeling. This does not mean I am stupid but just that sometimes it takes me longer to process what you are asking me and formulate the answer in my head before I speak out loud. Occasionally, I may not be able to speak to you at all, but again, this doesn't mean I am not intelligent, not listening or ignoring you. Just that I am wondering if, when I do speak, I am going to say the right thing, be heard or gaslighted into thinking I am the problem, as usually happens.

I often find it really difficult to communicate with people I don't know or when they expect me to communicate in a neurotypical way and don't try to understand the way I think and speak. It is difficult for me to understand what you are saying, especially when I cannot pick up clues from your gestures and tone of voice.

I have an excellent vocabulary but often struggle to find the right words or put them together coherently in a way that you might understand when being asked to do it verbally and at speed. I also worry and get anxious about my eye contact, tone of voice and the rules of social communication and how I am coming across to you when we are communicating. I may not know if or when to say something in a conversation and this may come across as rude but I am just anxious and thinking hard about what to say and when to say it.

Things that do *not* help me:

- putting me on the spot and expecting a quick answer
- not listening to how *I* feel and thinking my point of view is not valid because I have communication needs
- getting cross with me if I cannot interpret your facial expressions and body language
- slowing down your speech so much because you think I am stupid
- trying to change me to fit with the neurotypical way of communicating.

Things that *do* help me:

- giving me time to think and process
- validating how I am thinking and feeling
- letting me say things my own way then checking you have understood correctly if you are not sure
- explaining yourself clearly and giving as much detail as you can as I may take things literally – it also helps here if you give

- me lists or bullet points to work from in case I forget what you have said
- helping and supporting me to put my thoughts into sentences if I am struggling
- saying my name if you are speaking directly to me so I know you are talking to me
- letting me go somewhere quiet at lunchtime and break times so my brain can have a rest
- not expecting me to look at you when I am speaking as this makes it even more difficult for me to talk
- letting me write things down instead of speaking, which may be easier for me.

OVERVIEW OF NEEDS

Speech, language and communication needs (SLCN) should always be on your radar. But I appreciate that, as teachers or parents/carers of secondary school-aged children, they may not be.

As a former secondary science teacher (and secondary SENDCo), I've been there. I've flicked through my class lists, looked at the SEN register and presumed, based on the information in front of me, that I didn't have many students with SLCN in my classes. I also, perhaps naively (unless they had a diagnosed SLCN), presumed that by the time most children reach Year 7 and step into a secondary classroom, their speech, language and communication skills would be pretty much fully developed. In fact, I would have looked at this chapter and thought it wasn't that relevant to me. I was wrong.

Wrong because we know from research that ten per cent of students are affected by long-term and persistent speech, language and communication needs (Public Health England, 2020). And apologies for stating the obvious here, but just to emphasise my point, that's three students in every class of 30. If on a Monday, for example, you teach five periods of different classes of 30 students, you're teaching at least 15 students that day with SLCN. They may not be on your SEN register and they may not have been identified by anyone as having a SLCN. They could be hidden in clear view. Research shows us that 40 per cent of young people with SLCN are unidentified (The Communication

Trust, 2015). And if they've reached secondary school without their needs being noticed, they have likely developed (consciously or subconsciously) some incredible coping strategies that make it even trickier for us to identify them. But, identify and support them we must.

Putting in place strategies for SLCN in secondary school isn't just beneficial to those with SLCN but can be helpful for all students. This is because speech, language and communication skill development doesn't stop at primary school; students continue to develop these skills throughout secondary school too.

Speech, language and communication skills are fundamental, not just for academic success (they underpin literacy skill development for starters), but difficulties with these skills can impact on a student's behaviour, their friendships and overall wellbeing.

But before we look at how common speech, language and communication needs are and how you can identify students and support them, let's first unpick what we mean by speech, language and communication. Often, these terms are incorrectly used interchangeably, but they are discreet terms that have different meanings. This is important to note when we are identifying and supporting a student with a difficulty in one of these areas. The support for a student with a difficulty with their speech, for example, may look very different to the support given to a student who has a language skills difficulty.

USEFUL DEFINITION

SPEECH

Speech is the physical way we use sounds to form words. It encompasses articulation, which is how clearly we form distinct speech sounds. It also includes voice, fluency, and our ability to vary the volume, pitch and intonation of speech to support its meaning.

USEFUL DEFINITION

LANGUAGE

Language means a shared system or method of communication that has set rules. It can be spoken languages such as English, Spanish or Mandarin. Or non-spoken languages such as

British Sign Language (BSL). Language skills are divided into two categories: expressive language and receptive language. Expressive language is the 'output' of language: it's when we are communicating with others (through words, signs, symbols or written text); whereas receptive language is understanding what is being communicated to us.

USEFUL DEFINITION

COMMUNICATION

Communication is all about the interaction between people and the sharing of information. We can communicate in a whole range of ways, not just speaking. Students may communicate through writing, technology (phones and social media), assistive technology and sign language. Teenagers stereotypically use a lot of non-verbal communication, with body language, gestures and facial expressions. But we as teachers and/or parents/carers also use this form of communication – a disappointed look, a raised eyebrow or maybe even a huge smile (depending on our day!).

While speech, language and communication all have different meanings, it's imperative to remember that speech, language and communication *skills* are linked. A student who has difficulties with speech, may also have challenges with their language skills, for example.

WHAT ARE SPEECH, LANGUAGE AND COMMUNICATION NEEDS (SLCN)?

As explained previously, all students, regardless of whether they have SEND or not, will be continuing to develop their speech, language and communication skills throughout their secondary school years. They may be broadening their vocabulary, for example, learning to adapt their communication based on their audience, developing their skills in explaining and persuading, or learning to articulate when speaking in front of the class/school.

But for some students these skills may be more difficult to develop due to a SLCN. This could be a specific SLCN (diagnosed or undiagnosed) or a SLCN related to another SEND, such as autism.

SLCN cover a whole range of different needs. Some types of SLCN can be transient; others are lifelong. The majority may be identified in primary but there will also be some students whose SLCN only becomes clear in secondary school – sometimes due to the increased language demands of secondary school years.

There will also be some students whose SLCN appear to resolve during primary school, only to 'return' during secondary. This 'illusory recovery' is also more likely to be due to the increased language demands in secondary school making their SLCN more identifiable.

SLCN don't just include students who are finding speech difficult; it also includes (but is not limited to) students who find understanding (receptive) language more challenging and students who have difficulties with social communication skills. As some SLCNs can be transient, there will also be students in your classes who have had a SLCN but may not be impacted as much by it now. It might however, have had a lasting impact on other areas such as their literacy skills or even their self-esteem.

WHAT DOES SLCN INCLUDE?

- **Situational mutism** – This is an anxiety-based mental health disorder that causes students to be unable to speak in certain situations when they can speak happily and fluently in other situations. It can be thought of as a 'speech phobia'. You may find a student is able to speak at home but not in school. Or perhaps they are able to speak with some teachers but not others, etc. Situational Mutism (SM) is often referred to as 'Selective Mutism', but because the phrase 'selective' wrongly implies that the person has control over when they are able to speak/not speak, many people like myself prefer to use the term 'situational mutism'. It is thought that SM affects around one in 140 children and young people (NHS, 2023b). Without early intervention, SM can persist into the secondary school years and adulthood.

- **Stammer** – A stammer is when someone finds it difficult to speak in a smooth and fluent way. Stammering is also called stuttering or dysfluency. According to STAMMA, the British Stammering Association, eight per cent of children will start to stammer at some point and one per cent of adults stammer (n.d.).

- **Speech sound disorder and delays** – Speech sound disorders and delays involve difficulties with articulation (making the correct speech sounds) or phonology (using the sounds correctly). While these can be significantly improved with early identification and

Speech and Language Therapy (SaLT), speech sound disorders and delays can persist into adolescence. The difference between disorder and delay is that, unlike a speech disorder where a young person's progression of speech is on a different trajectory, a child or young person with a speech delay is on the same trajectory in terms of progression of their speech sounds but they are just taking longer than their peers.

- **Verbal dyspraxia** – This is a speech disorder. A student will usually know what they want to say but may be unable to physically make and coordinate the movements needed by their mouth to make the correct sounds.

- **Language disorders** – Language disorders are an umbrella term for a range of lifelong difficulties that impact language. They can be linked to other special educational needs and disabilities such as autism, or conditions such as brain injury.

- **Developmental language disorder** – One type of language disorder is called Developmental Language Disorder (DLD), previously known as Specific Language Impairment (SLI). DLD affects 7.58 per cent of students (Norbury et al., 2016) therefore in a class of 30 there will be at least two students with DLD. However, many children and young people with DLD are 'missed' and not identified as having DLD. This is despite DLD being much more common than autism. The criteria for DLD diagnosis is that a student has language difficulties that impact everyday life, that these language difficulties are unlikely to/haven't been resolved by the age of five and their difficulties aren't associated with a known biomedical condition (e.g. a brain injury or genetic disorder). DLD also impacts other areas of school, for example, 50 to 90 per cent of children with DLD have reading difficulties (Stothard et al., 1998). DLD can co-occur with dyslexia, speech sound disorder and ADHD.

- **Language delay** – A language delay is when a student's language progresses on the same trajectory as their peers, but slower. Unlike language disorders, in many cases with the correct support, language delay isn't lifelong.

- **Voice problems** – These refer to any problems that impact a student's voice. This could be voice loss, problems with the quality of voice or a hoarse voice, for example.

- **Social communication difficulties** – Social communication is simply how we use verbal and non-verbal communication socially. We use these skills to form, develop and maintain relationships. Young people who have difficulties with social communication skills may have difficulties with either verbal and non-verbal communication (or both). Young people may find it difficult to know when it's their turn in a conversation or activity. They may find it difficult to 'read' facial expressions and may find concepts and unwritten rules such as 'personal space' challenging to understand. Students can also experience difficulties with pragmatics – varying the way they speak or communicate in different circumstances. For example, speaking in a different way, with different use of language to teachers and parents/carers, compared to their peers. They may struggle to know how to change aspects of speech such as the volume, tone of voice or pitch in different situations. At primary school this may have been less apparent or not caused as many problems, but when students reach secondary school there are often more significant differences in the way students communicate to their peers compared to teachers. Students may also find non-literal language and idioms difficult, such as 'it's raining cats and dogs'. Changes to their routine, break times and other unstructured/less structured situations may also be more challenging.

OTHER CONSIDERATIONS

Overlap with other types of SEND

As with other areas of need, speech, language and communication needs often (although not always) overlap with other types of SEND. It's worth remembering that, although a student's primary need on the SEN register could be SLCN, they may co-occur with other SEND (and vice versa). And perhaps even more important to remember is that if they don't have SLCN as their primary area of need but have one of these SEND listed below, they may also have SLCN. These include, although are not limited to:

- **Autism** – Autistic students' speech, language and communication needs vary and are unique to the autistic individual. Some autistic students may have difficulties with receptive (understanding) language and/or expressive (using) language. A key diagnostic criterion for an autism diagnosis is difficulties in social communication and social interaction.

- **Social, Emotional and Mental Health (SEMH) difficulties** – Not only does there appear to be an overlap with SEMH and SLCN, but many children who we may have identified as having SEMH needs may, in fact, have unmet SLCN. Studies show that eight in ten children with 'emotional and behaviour disorders' have unidentified language difficulties (Hollo et al., 2014). Therefore,

I would urge you to screen students with SEMH for hidden, unidentified SLCN. I would also recommend looking at the student's primary area of need that was identified in primary school and check if it was SLCN but has now been changed to SEMH!

▶ **Dyslexia** – Many children with SLCN also have dyslexia. Fifty-one per cent of students with DLD, for example, are also dyslexic (Adlof & Hogan, 2018).

▶ **Attention Deficit Hyperactivity Disorder (ADHD)** – ADHD can sometimes impact on a whole range of language skills. Students may have difficulties with expressive (using) language, receptive (understanding) language and pragmatic language (using language socially).

▶ **Developmental Coordination Disorder (DCD)** – DCD, sometimes known as dyspraxia, can make the planning and coordination of movements more difficult. As a result, it can make using the correct words and producing the correct speech sounds difficult.

Hearing loss or deafness

▶ Hearing loss or deafness can affect a student's speech, language and communication, resulting in speech, language and communication difficulties and/or delays. In the UK, there are more than 50,000 deaf children (most taught in mainstream schools). Nine per cent of these children use British Sign Language (BSL) to communicate (Oracy Education Commission, 2024).

English as an Additional Language (EAL)

▶ EAL is not a SLCN, or a cause of SLCN – quite the opposite. In fact, there are massive cognitive advantages to speaking more than one language. There will, of course, be students who have English as an additional language and also a SLCN, as ten per cent of *all* students are affected by long-term and persistent speech, language and communication needs. If you are unsure if a student with EAL may have SLCN, speak to their family to find out if they are having difficulties with their home language in addition to their English.

WHY ARE SPEECH, LANGUAGE AND COMMUNICATION SKILLS IMPORTANT?

Speech, language and communication skills are important for all children and young people. But there are unique challenges for students with SLCN when they reach secondary school, one of which being the increased vocabulary demands put upon students. Oxford Education Language Group (2020) found that children and young people in Year 7 are exposed to three to four times as many new words per day as those in Year 6.

Students also have to navigate a busier environment, more complex social language, more demanding subject specific vocabulary, new vocabulary that has different meanings in different lessons and input from several different teachers in one day (instead of one/two at primary). They also need to use their language skills to negotiate, persuade, justify and solve problems.

While at primary school, the impacts of SLCN are huge and include behaviour, literacy barriers and difficulties forming and maintaining friendships, at secondary school we are also looking at impacts on GCSEs, job prospects, mental health issues, social isolation and even vulnerability to criminality. I cannot stress enough the importance of supporting students' SLCN.

Effects of unsupported SLCN include:

- **Social impact** – Friendships and relationships are important for students' wellbeing, especially so in secondary school. Difficulties with speech, language and communication skills can make it harder for some students to form, develop and maintain friendships. This can be due to difficulties expressing their thoughts, difficulties understanding others speaking (receptive language difficulties) or challenges with social communication skills. Research has shown that students with DLD, for example, were more likely to be isolated and had significantly smaller friendship groups than students without DLD (Chen et al., 2020). Friendships are arguably important for all students' mental health and wellbeing, but it has been shown that better relationships with peers can offer protection against mental health difficulties for teenagers with DLD (Forrest et al., 2018).

- **Mental health** – Having speech, language and communication needs can negatively impact students' self-esteem and mental health, perhaps even more so in secondary, where students are likely to be much more aware and self-conscious of their SLCN. Students with SLCN, particularly with language difficulties, have been shown to have higher levels of anxiety than their peers (Botting et al., 2016).

- **Academic success** – SLCN can affect a student's academic success. Studies have found that children who were identified as having persistent speech difficulties aged eight, had poor educational attainment at ages 10–11 and 13–14 years in the core subjects (English, maths and science) (Wren et al., 2021). Also, 20 per cent of students with SLCN gain grade 4 or above in English and maths at GCSE, compared with 64 per cent of all students (Public Health England, 2020). The reasons behind the impact of SLCN on academic success will be multifaceted and individual to each unique learner. However, we know that SLCN can have a significant impact on literacy skills (50–90 per cent of students with persistent SLCN will go on to have literacy difficulties) (Stothard, 1998) and good literacy skills are fundamental to accessing the curriculum (Dockrell et al., 2007). Good vocabulary knowledge, for example, is linked to higher exam success at GCSE (Croll, 1995). Ofsted has also said that: 'Where inspectors saw links between oral language, reading and writing in lessons with secondary school students, standards at GCSE English language were higher' (Ofsted, 2011).

- **Employment** – The ramifications of unsupported SLCN on academic success don't just stop in the secondary classroom, but can lead to potential unemployment. Speech and Language UK (2023) estimated that 'Children who struggle to talk and understand words are twice as likely to be unemployed'.

- **Behaviour** – It must be incredibly frustrating being a student with SLCN in the classroom. Perhaps even more so if it hasn't been identified. Imagine not being able to express your thoughts clearly, finding instructions difficult to follow or being worried about other's responses to the sound/fluency of your speech. This frustration can understandably impact a student's behaviour. In fact, 81 per cent of children with 'emotional and behaviour disorders have significant unidentified communication needs' (RCSLT, 2019). In terms of students whose SLCN *have* been identified, studies have shown that they have an 'elevated risk of social, emotional and behavioural difficulties in adolescence' (Snowling et al., 2006). In addition to this, two-thirds of students who are classed as 'at risk' of exclusion from school have been shown to have language difficulties (Clegg et al., 2009).

- **Behaviour outside of school** – Difficulties with behaviour, as we know, do not just impact on school life, but outside of school, too. According to The Centre for Social Justice, if unsupported, over 50 per cent of children with communication needs may become involved in criminal activity (2014). And research on language skills of a sample of juvenile offenders, showed 66–90 per cent of them had below-average language skills (Bryan et al., 2007).

WHAT YOU MIGHT NOTICE

As you'll be aware, as teachers, SENDCos or parents/carers we are not qualified to diagnose students with a SLCN, therefore the list below should not be used as a checklist to make assumptions about a student. However, while we can't diagnose, we *are* the first point of call and the ones who will be part of a referral to a speech and language therapist if needed, so it's useful to have an idea of what students who have a SLCN might potentially find difficult. Please remember that all students are unique and as such will not present in the same way.

SPEECH

Students may:

- have a stammer
- have a lisp
- have difficulties pronouncing certain sounds or certain words (particularly those with more than one syllable)
- omit particular sounds in words
- not talk at all, or very much, or limit who they speak to
- only use certain words (ones that they are confident they can produce clearly)
- find group work difficult
- have a small friendship group of trusted friends.

EXPRESSIVE LANGUAGE

Students may:

- talk very little and limit where and when they speak, and who they speak to (they may prefer to speak to a teaching assistant (TA) instead of the teacher, for example, and they may appear to struggle with group/paired work when they are not grouped with their friends)
- start explaining something or retelling an event and then give up
- struggle to resolve conflicts with their peers verbally
- use words in the incorrect context
- find it difficult to put words into a sentence and/or speak in shorter sentences than their peers. As a general guide, The Communication Trust (2015) explains that the average length of spoken words by age 11 is seven to 11+ words and seven to 12+ words aged 13/14.

VOCABULARY

Students may:

- have a limited vocabulary
- have difficulty in remembering, understanding and using new subject-specific vocabulary (this can be particularly difficult for Key Stage 4 students who will be expected to use and give definitions of subject-specific words)
- find it difficult to understand how some words have different meanings in different subjects/contexts.

RECEPTIVE LANGUAGE

Students may:

- need help understanding and following verbal instructions (a student may appear to be misbehaving and purposefully doing the opposite to what you have asked, when in fact they have misunderstood the verbal instruction)
- also notice that they just follow the last part of an instruction that they heard (according to the Communications Trust (2013), by Year 7, most students should be able to follow complex instructions given verbally and by Key Stage 4, should be able to follow complex instructions even if they aren't in the right order).

SOCIAL COMMUNICATION

Students may:

- have difficulties forming, developing and maintaining friendships – they may have arguments with their peers due to social misunderstandings and may have a small group of trusted friends
- find it difficult to understand other people's viewpoints – this can lead to confusion, arguments with peers and difficulties with some lessons that require students to write about or discuss different views
- misunderstand gestures, body language and personal space – this may result in difficulties and arguments with their peers
- take things literally
- difficulties with using inference skills
- not (always) understand/be able to use sarcasm and double meanings – you would expect most children starting Year 7 without a SLCN to be able to start to understand sarcasm, especially if we emphasised it, e.g. when something expected happens, saying

'well *that* was a surprise', and by Key Stage 4 they should be quite adept at spotting sarcasm
▶ need help to follow 'unwritten' social rules, such as adapting the choice of language for the situation/audience. This can impact both relationships with teachers (getting into trouble for not speaking politely enough to a member of staff) and peers (not keeping up with slang, or speaking too formally with peers).

OTHER CONSIDERATIONS

Behaviour

It is worth noting that difficulties with speech, language and communication aren't as easy to identify at secondary school and may be identified as 'problems with behaviour' instead of SLCN. Ofsted reported that sometimes children's SLCN is being misinterpreted; some students 'were allocated support for their behaviour when, in fact, they had specific communication needs' (Ofsted, 2010). In my experience, students at secondary school with SLCN develop a range of (self-made) coping strategies to hide/mask and deal with their needs. Some of these strategies are helpful and others are not. This may be a result in being self-conscious of their SLCN and trying to keep their needs quiet from their peers. As a result, students with speech, language and communication difficulties may tick very few of the boxes above but instead, students may:

▶ have brilliant visual strengths
▶ whisper instructions to themselves after they've been given them, as a strategy to help themselves remember and process the instruction easier
▶ appear disengaged
▶ take longer than their peers to start the work or follow a class instruction
▶ quietly concentrate on their written work (to blend in)
▶ rely on a friend during lesson times, copy others or watch the response of others first before reacting – for example, if you ask the class to line up by the door, they might watch what their peers do first before doing it themselves
▶ use made-up words in place of real ones they don't know, for example, 'word book' instead of 'dictionary'
▶ misbehave, make jokes or distract (to redirect the focus from their difficulties) – they may ask for equipment, for example, or ask you a question to take away the focus from them answering a question

- have poor behaviour and/or attendance. A student's behaviour may have deteriorated since primary school – this may be because their language skills were 'good enough' at primary school, and therefore weren't identified but, as a result of the additional language demands of secondary school, they may start to find lessons more challenging. And their needs may become more apparent.

Echolalia

- Students, especially some autistic students, may use echolalia in their communication. Echolalia is the repetition of words, often someone else's words from daily life or a TV programme. These phrases may appear at first to have no meaning, but often if you listen closely they do. For example, if a student who uses echolalia always hears someone on TV say 'Don't forget your coat' when they go outside, they may start to say 'don't forget your coat' instead of asking if it's time to go outside. It's worth tuning into the phrases any student who communicates with echolalia uses and speaking to their family to work out the meaning of that phrase for them.

STRATEGIES

Here are some strategies for both school and home to help students develop their speech, language and communication skills. If a student has a diagnosed SLCN or a particular SEND that impacts on their speech, language and communication skills and they receive support from an external professional, ensure you are implementing their suggestions of strategies.

IN THE CLASSROOM

These strategies are designed specifically for the classroom, suitable for both teachers and teaching assistants. I've split these strategies into three sections: one to give ideas of how to provide more opportunities to practise speech, another with strategies to support speech and language and, finally, a section on supporting social communication skills.

SPEECH

- **Ask, don't presume** – Ask students (discreetly) what you can do to help support them in lessons. SLCN are broad and every student is unique, so don't assume you know how to support them based on their profile or diagnosis.

- **Be open if you don't understand something they say** – If you're finding it difficult to understand what a student is saying, perhaps due to a speech disorder/delay, don't pretend to understand but be patient and ask for clarification. A student is likely to be very aware if you pretend to understand what they've said.

- **Model good speech** – Students will learn a lot about speech, language and communication skills from observing us. Therefore, ensure you are modelling good speech. Be clear and concise when addressing the class, choose words carefully and ensure the volume and speed of your speech is appropriate. This will also be helpful for students with receptive language difficulties, aiding with their understanding of what you are saying. As Madison explains in the case study at the start of this chapter, it's really important not to speak too slowly as this can feel patronising and condescending.

- **Use names** – To help students with receptive language difficulties in particular, use their name at the start of any individual instructions.

- **Be sensitive and supportive about public speaking** – Students with a SLCN (identified or not) may find speaking in front of the class even more daunting than their peers but there are many things we can do to help. First and foremost, a whole classroom ethos of support and understanding is key to ensuring students feel safe speaking in front of others. Students with SLCN need to be certain that they won't be laughed at or teased by their peers for mispronunciation, stuttering or using the wrong words. Be positive, praise and model the response you expect from the rest of the class.

- **Be flexible with public speaking** – This might be providing opportunities for students to speak in front of a small group first/instead. Or it may be enabling them to practise with a member of staff in advance, before addressing the whole class. The support needed will be unique to each student; ask them about their preferences and how best to support them.

- **Careful correction** – Be careful not to knock a student's confidence in their own speech. If they make an error when speaking, don't jump in to correct, but repeat the phrase back to them with encouragement and with the correction embedded. For example, 'I buyed a new iPhone at the weekend'. Instead of saying 'No, it's *bought* not buyed' say 'Oh fantastic, you *bought* a new iPhone at the weekend... Tell me more about it'.

▶ **Speaking frame** – Just as a writing frame supports students to organise their written work, a speaking frame helps to organise what they are going to say. This could be written or presented as visuals; it could also be created in co-production with the student. It provides them with sentence starters and structure for providing verbal answers. You could also consider using one to support a child with informal speaking – such as conversations between peers or asking for help from a teacher. (Please note that, as with any social support, it must not be forced upon the young person and instead offered as advice if the young person is asking for help.)

LANGUAGE

▶ **Give time** – The Communication Trust (2015) recommends allowing ten seconds for students to think of the answer to a question. This is particularly beneficial for students with receptive language difficulties, but will also aid in improving the quality of their verbal answers. Time to think of answers is not the only thing to consider; we also need to allow time for students to speak (without pressure and interruptions).

▶ **Say what you will say, say it and then say what you said** – There's no catchy way to describe this! Look at the structure of your *own* speech and provide students with information about what you are going to say, as well as a summary afterwards. This can help students to retain instructions more easily, especially if they have difficulties with receptive language skills.

▶ **Speak to a partner** – Enabling time for students to speak to a partner, to discuss their ideas before answering a question in front of the class, can help to build self-esteem and improve the quality of verbal answers. Don't presume students will know how to utilise this support effectively; you may decide to provide cues or structure for some students so they can get the most out of this – perhaps using visuals. For example, you could give the following sentence starters for discussion: 'My opinion is… because…', ' Good point, but what about…' and 'Overall we've agreed that…'.

▶ **Chunking** – Just as you might chunk long written text into smaller sections with breaks to support a student with literacy difficulties, support language difficulties by chunking speech. Provide verbal information in smaller bitesize chunks with pauses to allow students to process the information. This is particularly helpful for students with receptive language difficulties.

- **Consider instructions** – Provide clear instructions. Start instructions with the student's name and ensure the instructions aren't overly 'wordy' and are in the correct order. For example, 'Oliver, please could you hand out the books, then get your pen out and write today's title and date' is much easier to follow than 'We'll need to write today's title and date, so please could you hand out the books and get your pen out'.

- **Think about questions** – Just like instructions, questions should start with the student's name and be free of any unnecessary words. Try to avoid rhetorical questions; these can be particularly confusing for some neurodivergent students, for example, who may take language literally.

- **Provide vocabulary for clarification** – Not only do we need to provide subject-specific vocabulary, but we also need to give students vocabulary to be able to ask for clarification and check their understanding. This vocabulary could be displayed on the board or provided as 'keyword mats'. You could also model using clarification questions yourself when checking your own understanding of answers given, and emphasise and praise others who are using this vocabulary. In addition, creating a safe environment in your classroom where students feel confident to ask if they don't understand something is key.

- **Reduce background noise** – Many students with SLCN will benefit from a reduction in background noise, especially students with receptive language difficulties. A quieter and less distracting classroom environment enables students to process the language they have heard more easily. Background noise isn't just other students talking, but it can be anything from the noise of other classes outside doing PE to the hum of the projector. Students with sensory differences may also be more aware and sensitive to noises that we may not have realised were a problem. Speaking to the student and carrying out a sensory audit can be helpful (see Chapter 5).

- **Talk less** – School can be very 'language heavy' for teenagers in particular; not only are they navigating more complex vocabulary in the classroom but they are also immersed in more informal language (slang) at break time. For students with language difficulties, this can make the school day particularly exhausting. One way we can help is to simply talk less by being more concise when addressing the class.

- **Think about your position in the classroom** – Make it easier for students to hear and understand what you are saying, and to lip-read if needed, by considering where you stand when addressing the class. For example, if you often stand in front of a window, you will be backlit making it harder for students to see your mouth. Also, think about how the classroom is organised; are you facing *all* the students or just some?

▶ **Pre-teach vocabulary** – Students need to learn a lot of complex vocabulary at secondary school, some of which is subject-specific. One way to support students with SLCN (and all students!) with the acquisition of these new words is to pre-teach. Provide them with the key words and definitions in advance of the lesson.

▶ **Teach vocabulary explicitly** – Give definitions, use repetition, link new words to other words in different subjects and support with visuals. Enabling students to create their own visuals for keywords can also be helpful.

▶ **Vocabulary games** – These can be as part of the lesson if time allows or set as homework. Games to help learn new vocabulary include matching games (match the definition to the word), key word bingo (they write down six of the keywords, read out the definitions, if it is their word they cross it off, first one to cross all words off wins), charades, hangman, Pictionary.

▶ **Mind maps** – Teach students to use mind maps to summarise new vocabulary, links between words and their definitions with a mind map.

▶ **Voice note instruction/jot it down** – For some students, as Madison describes in the case study, it can be helpful to provide a summary of the task instruction. This can be particularly helpful to students with receptive language difficulties who might find processing language more challenging. There are lots of ways you can do this, and I'd advise asking the student for their preference. One way can be to record the instruction as a voice note (if you have the tech available). Another way is simply to write down a summary of the instructions for that student. If you have a TA in the lesson, they may be able to do this as part of the support they provide.

▶ **Label equipment** – Labelling equipment, resources and trays can be particularly helpful for students with language difficulties (especially with visuals). Verbal instructions given to students to go and find a resource/equipment can be difficult for some children with language processing difficulties, and this can be compounded if they then have to work out where the equipment is. Therefore, labelling takes away/reduces this additional cognitive demand.

SOCIAL COMMUNICATION

USEFUL DEFINITIONS

Neurodiversity – The variety between how different people's brains work.

Neurodivergence – When the way someone's brain works, processes and thinks diverges from societal norms. People who are neurodivergent might be autistic, have ADHD, dyslexia, dyscalculia, dysgraphia or Developmental Coordination Disorder (DCD), for example.

Neurotypical – Someone who is neurotypical, on the other hand, is said to think and process information in a 'typical' way according to the societal norms.

Masking – When someone consciously or subconsciously hides their true self and feelings in order to 'fit in' and meet social (neurotypical) expectations. Masking can be exhausting and hugely detrimental to their mental health and wellbeing.

NEUROAFFIRMATIVE APPROACH

Social communication skills enable students to form and maintain friendships, resolve conflicts, develop confidence, interact with others, solve problems and develop life skills – making them an important skill set to support students to develop.

However, we must be careful when supporting students to develop their social communication skills that we are being neuro-affirming. That is to say, we aren't trying to change a neurodivergent person to act 'more neurotypical'. This could result in a neurodivergent student masking, where they subconsciously or consciously hide their true self to fit in, often at great expense to their own wellbeing.

One example of being neuro-affirming, explained beautifully in the case study by Madison, is not insisting on eye contact from someone. Certain students for example, some autistic students find giving eye contact uncomfortable (sometimes painful). It's vital for their wellbeing that we respect this. It would also be counterintuitive for us to insist on it, as a student may use so much energy trying to give us eye contact that they may not be able to concentrate properly on the lesson/instruction.

This may also be the same for some students who find sitting still, without fidgeting, difficult. If we insist on sitting still at all times, they may not be able to concentrate on the lesson. Whereas, if we were more neuro-affirming and provided them with movement opportunities, they may be able to get the most out the lesson.

We also must ensure that any social communication support for students is what *they* want, not what *we* think they should be doing. It could be argued that many social skills strategies, if insisted upon, are ableist as they are only taking into account neurotypical ways of communication.

For example, a student may choose to sit outside every lunchtime and read a book, instead of interacting with their peers. While we may feel keen to support them in developing skills to interact with their peers at lunchtime, they may be very happy reading and do not want to mix with their peers at lunchtime. In which case, it would be inappropriate to insist on strategies for them to interact with their peers at lunchtime. However, if a student was struggling with a particular friendship and *asked* for tips to help resolve a conflict, that would be an appropriate time to provide some useful strategies that they could *choose* to use.

Social communication support strategies in lessons could include:

- **Structuring group work** – Some students may benefit from more structure in group work situations. This could include providing set roles within the group with explanations of what each member of the group's role is. You could also provide guidance on how to work well as a group, what sort of things people say to one another to get their ideas across well and how to resolve disagreements. Modelling this in front of the class could be particularly helpful.

- **Providing explanations for unwritten rules** – Don't presume all students understand unwritten rules. Unwritten rules include: how to take your turn in conversations, not boasting about academic success and how we speak differently to our peers as opposed to a member of staff. Support students with these unwritten rules by explaining them and the reasons we have them.

- **Teach idioms** – If you use idioms in a lesson, such as 'it's raining cats and dogs outside', explain it afterwards. For many neurodivergent students, idioms are a particularly difficult concept.

ACROSS THE SCHOOL

While teachers can use strategies in the classroom to support children with SLCN, having a school-wide approach as well (led by the SENDCo and/or SLT) may enable more consistency. I've purposefully not split these strategies into speech, language and communication categories as many of them span more than one area.

- **Whole-school audit** – Auditing your provision for identifying and supporting students with SLCN as well as whole-school strategies for speech, language and communication skill development should be encouraged.

- **After-school/lunchtime clubs to promote and practise speech, language and communication** – After-school or lunchtime clubs can be a fantastic 'opt-in' way to develop young people's speech, language and communication skills in a small group while having fun with their friends. Examples of clubs that would be useful for the development of these skills include: school radio/podcasting club, debating club, sign language club, singing club, book club and LEGO® Club. However, any club that is set up in a way that enables communication between students in a relaxed way will be beneficial. Please be very mindful of any 'social skills' groups, interventions or clubs. Groups and clubs need to be neuro-affirming, by that I mean we must make sure we're not trying to change a neurodivergent student to act 'more neurotypical'. This can result in a student masking (which is where they consciously or subconsciously hide their true self in order to fit in). Masking can be detrimental to a young person's mental health and wellbeing. Groups/clubs need to not focus solely on the 'neurotypical way' of communication, but be accepting of other ways too. Social skill groups that are opt in, and provide helpful tips about navigating social situations, can be helpful if done sensitively.

- **Raise the profile of speech, language and communication skills** – This could be via staff CPD. You could also have a specific speech, language and communication focus each week/month across the school, sharing approaches, research and activities.

- **School ethos of 'vocab learners'** – There are lots of ways you can do this, for example, ensuring vocabulary development is developed across the curriculum (not just in English), vocabulary is taught explicitly, there's a culture of reading, a vocabulary-rich school environment and engagement with families on key vocabulary (this could be done through the school website/portal and newsletters).

- **Create a consistent approach to how vocabulary is introduced and taught across subjects** – The increased language demands of the secondary school curriculum mean that students have to learn a lot of new complex vocabulary in different subjects. Some of these words also have different meanings depending on the subject. Having a consistent approach to how new vocabulary is introduced and reinforced will help students with this.

- **Colour code classrooms based on subject** – Having signs on classroom doors that are colour coded, based on the subject, provides students with SLCN with a clear and concrete reference for that subject. It reduces cognitive load, as they don't need to remember which subject/teacher is in which classroom but can link the colour to that subject. It can be particularly helpful for students who may have receptive language difficulties and find processing verbal instructions more difficult, as it reduces how much information they need to process.

- **Opportunity to share good speech, language and communication skills practice** – There will be members of staff in your school who are fantastic at supporting students with SLCN within their lessons. Share this good practice. This could be through CPD, student voice, staff briefings and providing opportunities for staff to observe these strategies in action. If you're able to link up with your local special school to learn from them, this would be helpful too.

- **Quiet space available for study/regulation** – As Madison explained in the case study, some students benefit from having a quiet space in school to regulate their feelings and study. Ensure a suitable space is available in your school.

- **Acoustics of the classrooms** – Getting the acoustics of a classroom right is more important than most people realise. In fact, they can be crucial when students are trying to hear and process spoken language. This is even more so for students with a SLCN, where an echoey, noisy classroom can make it even more challenging. There are lots of simple ways you can improve the acoustics of the classrooms across your school, including soft furnishings, acoustic panelling and thinking about the arrangement of the classroom. If budget allows, there are also other options including soundproofing and speech amplification systems (these enable all students to hear the teacher clearly no matter where they are sitting).

- **Student voice** – Don't presume we have all the answers; speak to students and collect 'student voice' on what strategies are working for them and what more we can do to help. Not only does this better inform our support but it also gives students the agency and autonomy to speak up for themselves on what they need, which is a useful life skill to develop.

- **Support at break times** – Think about how you can support any students with social communication needs at break times. Unstructured time can sometimes be difficult. It may be that, alongside quiet areas for study, there are also more clubs at lunchtime and access to the library.

- **Promote self-advocacy** – Alongside support, we also want students to feel confident and able to advocate for themselves. This can only be done if there is a culture of understanding and teachers are able to respond positively to students advocating for themselves.

AT HOME

Young people don't just develop speech, language and communication skills at school and therefore the role of the young person's family is paramount. If you're a parent or carer reading this, these strategies might be helpful for supporting your child, but *you* have the expertise on your own child and their needs, so pick and choose which ones will work best. If you're a teacher/SENDCo, these could be strategies you share with the families of the students with SLCN you support. I've split these strategies into three sections: one to give ideas of how to provide more opportunities to practise speech, another with strategies to support speech and language and, finally, a section on supporting social communication skills.

PROVIDING OPPORTUNITIES FOR SPEECH

This is a complete generalisation, but teenagers are notorious for not being as keen to talk to their parents/carers as they might have done when they were younger. This can be particularly difficult if they have a SLCN and you're keen to develop their speech, language and communication skills. Instead of forcing interactions, work at providing more natural opportunities for speech, language and communication skill development. These could include:

- **Asking them to help you** – Find something that they are better at than you, and ask them to help you with it. This could be an app on your phone or a problem with your emails, for example. Make sure it is a genuine problem you need help with.

- **Creating opportunities for talking** – This might be car journeys, walking the dog together, helping with DIY or cooking together.

▶ **Family mealtime** – Mealtimes at the table as a family, while difficult to juggle with our busy lives, provide a brilliant opportunity for teenagers to practise speech and language skills in a safe space, without judgement. They are also brilliant for modelling social communication skills, such as taking turns in conversations.

▶ **Share some of their interests** – It is often easier to talk about something you care about, so whether it's gaming, TikTok or football – being genuinely engaged in their interests enables you to have common ground which you can talk about together (thus developing speech, language and communication skills).

SUPPORTING SPEECH AND LANGUAGE

▶ **Give them time** – This may be time to respond (process the information they have been given) or time to speak. Be patient, don't hurry them along or try to finish their sentences. Give them the time and space to develop these skills.

▶ **Use visuals** – Get into the habit of using visuals to help support their speech, language and communication skills. This could be using photographs. For example, if they are telling grandparents about what they did over the weekend – give them their/your phone with photos taken over the weekend as a prompt to help them retell the event.

▶ **Reduce background noise** – Easier said than done, but be mindful of background noise (TV, music, phone notifications, siblings) at home during times when they are speaking to you. Reducing these noises can help with their receptive (understanding) language skills, as well as their speech.

▶ **Model speech and language skills** – Share stories about your day. By doing this you are modelling how to retell a series of events – something that many young people with SLCN find challenging.

▶ **Talk about new words** – Try to get into the habit of discussing new words that you hear together on the TV. You could even jot them down, look up the meaning and challenge each other to try and use them (where appropriate!). It's also important to try to give them confidence to ask when they don't know what a word means. One way to help this is by asking *them* about a slang word that you don't know.

▶ **Watch family TV** – The quality of language teenagers are exposed to on social media, gaming and YouTube isn't often as good as the language on TV channels. Watching a film together might provide them with exposure to more useful vocabulary.

- **Support them with subject-specific vocabulary** – They will be learning lots of new words in all their different subjects in school. Speak to their teachers/SENDCo to ask to be sent new vocabulary that you can practise together at home.

- **Word puzzles** – Word puzzles, such as crosswords, are brilliant for broadening vocabulary.

SUPPORT SOCIAL COMMUNICATION SKILLS

- **Practise adapting language when speaking to different people** – For example, how we speak differently to a member of staff at school from how we speak to a peer. The type of vocabulary we might use and why.

- **Teach them about idioms and sarcasm** – If this is something they find difficult, explicitly teach them idioms and sarcasm. Point it out on TV when you're watching together, talk about it and use examples.

- **Allow them to ask you questions about new 'slang' and 'street talk'** – It's not just new vocabulary in lessons that teenagers have to learn, it's also slang and street talk that they learn to interact with their peers. Keep the door open for them to ask you about any new words they have heard and be open and honest about them. Help them to understand the meaning and how their peers use it in conversations to support them with friendships.

- **Consider suitable extracurricular activities** – Some extracurricular activities can be fantastic for developing social communication skills. Discuss together clubs such as youth clubs, scouts, sports clubs, etc.

RESOURCES

INTERVENTIONS AND PROGRAMMES

- **Blank's Levels of Questioning** – Created in the 1970s by Dr Blank and colleagues, this helps children and young people through four levels of questioning to develop language, comprehension and inference skills.

- **Colourful Semantics** – Developed by SaLT Alison Bryan, Colourful Semantics helps children and young people to understand how a sentence is formed through colour coding. Each part of the sentence has a set colour linked to a question. You can use Colourful Semantics to support speech and language by helping children to form sentences verbally and understand questions such as 'Where?', 'What?' and 'Who?'. It can also be used to help support literacy.

- **Talk for Work** – Previously called 'Talk about Secondary', this evidence-based intervention programme created by Speech and Language UK aims to help students aged 14–18 with difficulties in speech and language to prepare for the workplace.

- **LEGO® Therapy** – Founded by Daniel LeGoff, a psychologist, LEGO® therapy aims to support children and young people's development of social communication skills through LEGO® play. LEGO® therapy was initially developed with autistic children and young people in mind.

- **Secondary Language Link** – Created by Speech and Language Link, this intervention and assessment package is for students aged 11–14 with language and communication needs.

VISUAL SUPPORTS AND AAC SUPPORTS

- **DocsPlus** – This is a software programme designed for secondary-aged students to help them organise their ideas, increase vocabulary and create written tasks more independently. A full review of the software can be found on my website, The SEN Resources Blog www.senresourcesblog.com.

- **Twinkl Symbols** – This is a great tool for supporting students' communication with pictures. It enables you to create customised resources with picture symbols as well as download ready-made symbol resources. There is also a free app to download.

- **Choice boards** – Print images representing activities like 'reading', 'gaming' or 'football'. On a separate sheet of paper, create spaces where the images can be placed. This system can help non-speaking young people to communicate their choices and even arrange the activities by priority.

- **Communication boards** – These are a sheet of card with symbols/pictures on which students can point to as a way of communicating their emotions or needs. Core boards are a great example of these.

- **Now and Next boards** – These help students to understand what is happening now and what will happen next. They also enable them to communicate what they want to do now and later. They are simply a piece of card with the word 'now' written to the left and 'next' on the right. You or the student place pictures under each word to show what they are doing now and what they are doing next.

- **Visual timetable** – This is a useful tool for communicating with students about what will be happening during the day. These can be bought or made yourself using pictures.
- **Visual task plan** – This is a checklist with pictures that shows the stages of a task broken down in order, with a box that students can use to mark the completion of each section (with a tick or a stamp).

OTHER RESOURCES

- **BSL online free dictionary** – There are plenty of resources out there to support learning BSL. One free resource that I would recommend is the BSL online free dictionary by Sign BSL. Simply type in a word and it comes up with a video showing how to sign it.
- **Pukka Pad Vocab Book** – This A4 size notepad is designed for students to write down new words, their definitions and much more and is a lovely way of organising new subject-specific vocabulary at secondary school.

FURTHER READING AND SUPPORT

Websites

Breakthrough Britain 2015 www.centreforsocialjustice.org.uk/wp-content/uploads/2018/03/CSJJ2470_BB_2015_WEB.pdf

Raising Awareness of Developmental Language Disorder (RADLD) www.radld.org/about/dld

Selective Mutism Information and Research Association (SMiRA) www.selectivemutism.org.uk

Speech and Language Link www.speechandlanguage.link

Speech and Language UK www.speechandlanguage.org.uk

The Communication Trust's 'Universally Speaking - The ages and stages of children's communication development' www.fis.cityoflondon.gov.uk/asset-library/tct-univspeak-11-18.pdf

The Selective Mutism Resource Manual, RCLSLT www.rcslt.org/speech-and-language-therapy/clinical-information/selective-mutism/

CHAPTER 2
LITERACY SKILLS

CASE STUDY

NICOLA PLATT, A SEND SPECIALIST LEADER IN EDUCATION, WHO WAS DIAGNOSED WITH DYSLEXIA AND ADHD IN ADULTHOOD, REFLECTS ON HER EXPERIENCE OF BEING UNDIAGNOSED AT SCHOOL AND THE DIFFICULTIES SHE FACED WITH LITERACY.

Picture a regular 1990s comprehensive school: class size of around 18, mixed abilities, all from working-class, low socio-economic households, but all reasonably happy kids with great attendance. Being somewhat of a people pleaser, I wanted praise from the teachers, though I felt I didn't often receive it. My speaking and writing skills were always good, but concentrating on a piece of text was so incredibly difficult; I'd find myself peering around the classroom to see if everyone else was reading; they were. Why was it so hard for me to do the same? 'Concentrate on your work, Nicola!' the teachers would bellow, instantly filling me with shame and guilt. 'Too much chatter, Nicola!,' consolidating my utter embarrassment.

School reports said, 'Nicola is a chatterbox', 'Nicola needs to apply herself', 'She is a lovely girl but doesn't try hard enough in her times tables', 'Nicola is a worrier, but doesn't seem to worry about forgetting to pay attention', 'Must try harder'. Though none of them ever wondered why, or tried to provide any kind of support, heaven forbid!

I remember the absolute terror of having to read a sentence out loud; I'd be so focused on rehearsing it in my head over and over again, I wouldn't take anything else in. Trying to remain calm while stuttering and skipping words, all while reading in some emotionless, robotic voice, merely trying to get through it.

Fast forward to 2024, I've opted to undertake a degree (having avoided it for 20 years from fear of failure). I find myself on a Zoom call with an educational psychologist (through Disabled Students' Allowance), filled with the exact same embarrassment having to read two texts out loud and then answer questions based on the content. Not only can I not remember any detail but I am also unable to answer the questions. I burst into tears as the shame has turned to self-loathing, as I'm now an adult who 'must try harder'.

However, once the educational psychology report lands in my inbox, the shame and self-loathing start to melt away: 'The results of the assessment indicate that Nicola presents a profile indicative of specific learning difficulties'. My jaw drops. As I read further, it enlightens me about poor auditory short-term memory, mental manipulation abilities, reading speed, fluency and comprehension, plus presenting traits of ADD (Attention Deficit Disorder). Fast forward another four months and I have the diagnosis of combined ADHD to boot. Suddenly all the teacher comments from childhood make sense. I now feel valid, let down, frustrated and a little sad. Imagine if the teachers knew this back then. Maybe I wouldn't have put off doing a degree for so long.

I started my master's in SEND and Inclusion in September 2025. Who would have thought it?

CHAPTER 2 • LITERACY SKILLS ◀

OVERVIEW OF NEED

Literacy skills are fundamental to academic success in secondary school. The way students access the curriculum and are assessed on their skills and understanding is predominantly through reading and writing.

It goes without saying that due to the literacy demands across the secondary curriculum, literacy support should be the responsibility of every member of staff and department.

It's important to note that while we often refer to literacy skills as 'reading and writing', literacy skills also encompass being able to communicate effectively through speaking and listening. I would therefore urge you to read Chapter 1 on *Speech, language and communication skills* alongside this chapter to ensure you are fully supporting and meeting the needs of young people with literacy difficulties.

WHAT DO WE MEAN BY READING AND WRITING SKILLS?

READING

What is reading? Simply put, reading is looking at some text (or touching using braille) and being able to work out what it means. As Castles *et al.* (2018) explain it, succinctly: 'The goal of reading is to understand what has been read'. But despite it first appearing simple, it is anything but. Reading is a complex process that involves decoding, word reading, fluency, grammar and vocabulary.

But where does it start?

While at secondary school we may not teach many students to read from scratch, we are still supporting their reading and, therefore, I think as parents/carers or teachers of secondary-aged students it's very helpful to know how they have been taught to read at primary school.

The majority of students arriving in Year 7 will have been taught how to read in primary school using phonics.

Phonics comes with lots of new terms, which I've summarised in this box:

USEFUL DEFINITIONS

Phonemes – individual sounds. They are the smallest unit of sound in a language that can distinguish words from each other.

Graphemes – individual sounds/phonemes in written form.

Digraphs – two letters that make one sound, e.g. 'ch' and 'ai'.

Trigraphs – three letters that make one sound, e.g. 'igh'.

Phonics involves teaching children to recognise and use individual sounds, known as phonemes. When written, phonemes are represented by graphemes, which include single letters like 's', 'a' and 't'; digraphs (two letters making one sound), such as 'ch' and 'ai'; and trigraphs (three letters making one sound) like 'igh'. Children use these graphemes to decode unfamiliar words in texts.

They learn to spot these graphemes, sound them out and blend them to form words. As children improve, their reading becomes more fluent, characterised by accuracy, a natural pace (automaticity) and good intonation, expression and rhythm (prosody).

In England, mainstream state primary schools currently teach reading and writing using phonics, specifically Systematic Synthetic Phonics (SSP). However, phonics guidance varies across the UK. For instance, in Northern Ireland, it is not mandatory to teach children using SSP, but many schools incorporate it into a balanced reading program.

Different SSP teaching programmes are used in schools, and the Department for Education provides a list of validated programmes in their guidance publication 'Choosing a Phonics Teaching Programme' (see *Further Reading and Support*).

For students who are still learning to read at secondary, phonics is still important.

Shift from learning to read to reading to learn

As students progress through school, the emphasis shifts from learning to read to reading to learn. This means that there is an expectation for most students to have developed basic reading skills and now be able to use these skills to find information, and gain understanding from books and texts they read. Concerningly, research shows that some students do not have the reading skills they require to access the secondary curriculum (Ricketts et al., 2020; van der Kleij et al., 2023).

Reading becomes the way to learn information across subjects, enabling students to explore and understand more complex concepts, engage with diverse material and develop critical thinking skills. The ability to read and learn information from reading is crucial for success in subjects like history, science and geography, where students must analyse and comprehend various types of texts, from textbooks to primary source documents.

Students will also be expected to not only gather information but also to evaluate, interpret and apply what they read to solve problems, complete written tasks and participate in discussions.

WRITING

Writing, like reading, is a complex process; it's not as simple as just getting a pen on paper – it also doesn't have to be with a pen or paper! Writing requires students to use executive functions to plan what they are going to write, compose and organise it (using their ideas, vocabulary and sentence structure), transcribe it (thinking about their spelling and their handwriting/typing) and then check what they have written and make any changes.

Students may have difficulties in any one (or more) of these areas and the support provided must be tailored to their needs. For example, support for a student who has difficulties with handwriting will look very different to support for a student with limited vocabulary.

Given the wide scope of literacy skills, there is significant overlap between this chapter and others. For instance, if a young person in your care is having difficulty with handwriting, you will find helpful strategies and resources in the chapter on *Motor skills* (Chapter 4). If they are finding organising their ideas challenging, Chapter 7 on *Concentration and organisation skills* may also be useful.

WHY ARE LITERACY SKILLS IMPORTANT?

Just like SLCN in Chapter 1, the importance of literacy skills cannot be underestimated. I wrote in *SEND Strategies for the Primary Years* about the impact of difficulties with reading and/or writing on a primary-aged child's self-esteem, wellbeing, behaviour, happiness and friendships. But as you can appreciate, the impacts on secondary-aged students can be felt perhaps even further.

Literacy is fundamental for academic success, underpinning learning across the secondary curriculum. Students need literacy skills for numerous aspects of lessons, including but certainly not limited to reading texts (books, articles, research, opinions), writing essays and answers, expressing their ideas in written form and solving problems. In fact, research by GL Assessment in 2020 found that 'Children who are weak readers will struggle as much in maths and science at GCSE as they do in English and in arts subjects'.

Students are also assessed using their reading and writing skills in many subjects, for example, needing to apply their literacy skills to understand and answer exam questions. A student's reading or writing difficulties can therefore impact on their ability to successfully show their understanding in assessments and exams. If we look at reading, for example, a quarter of 15-year-olds have a reading age of 12 or below (GL Assessment, 2020), yet the reading age for GCSE exam papers is 15 years and 7 months.

The impact of literacy skills isn't just felt while at school, but consequently in life after school. Future employment opportunities, for example, can be impacted by literacy skills. Research has shown that 'The average worker in the UK with very low literacy will earn approximately 7.1 per cent less than if they had a basic level of literacy' (PBE, 2021). They also found that people with very poor literacy skills are twice as likely to be unemployed.

Literacy is also an important life skill needed for everyday life, from reading road names and completing important forms to sending a WhatsApp message to a friend. And the latter shouldn't be dismissed as trivial as it can have a direct impact on their relationships with their peers. Many students communicate with each other after school via messages and social media, which requires literacy skills.

Reading also broadens young people's opinions and understanding by exposing them to different cultures and perspectives. Through reading, they can learn about different traditions and viewpoints they might not have been aware of. This can help young people to be more empathetic and understanding of others, which can help break down stereotypes. In summary, reading is one way to help young people to appreciate the diversity and complexity of the world.

Reading and writing can also be wonderful hobbies for many young people, providing them with a screen-free (sometimes) way to relax. Reading enables escape to imaginative worlds and freedom to learn in depth about interests. Writing also provides a vehicle to express their thoughts and feelings freely. However, despite the obvious benefits of reading and writing, it's clear we need to be doing a better job at marketing it. Only 26.6 per cent of children and young people aged 8–18 said they enjoyed reading in their free time in 2025 (the lowest level since surveys began in 2005) (National Literacy Trust, 2025a) and just 10.4 per cent of children and young people aged 8 to 18 wrote something daily in their free time in 2025, a significant decrease from 19.3 per cent in 2023 (National Literacy Trust, 2025b).

WHO MIGHT NEED FURTHER SUPPORT WITH THEIR LITERACY SKILLS?

There is a whole range of SEND that may affect a young person's literacy skills. I stress 'may' as we must remember that all young people are unique and are certainly not defined by a SEND and as such, they will have their own individual strengths and challenges.

Generally speaking, if you have students in your class with (but not limited to) the specific SENDs listed below, or your own child has one of these special educational needs or disabilities, then they may have difficulties with some areas of literacy.

- **Dyslexia** – Most people will be aware that dyslexia can affect a person's reading and writing. But it also impacts on other skills, including their processing skills, organisation skills and working memory.
- **Visual stress/Irlen syndrome** – This isn't a problem with sight, vision or a person's eyes, but a difficulty with processing and making sense of visual information (see *Further Reading and Support*). There appear to sometimes (but not always) be overlaps between this and other SEND such as autism, ADHD and dyslexia.
- **SLCN** – As mentioned, there is a huge link between SLCN and literacy. It is therefore not a surprise that difficulties with speech, language and communication can make literacy more difficult. For further advice and strategies on this, see Chapter 1.
- **SEND that affect motor skills** – Difficulties with motor skills can impact on a young person's ability to write as well as their stamina when writing. Motor skill difficulties often impact on a young person's handwriting. SEND that affect motor skills include (but are not limited to): cerebral palsy, DCD (dyspraxia), dysgraphia and hypermobility. See Chapter 4 for further advice and strategies for difficulties with motor skills.

- **ADHD** – Some, but certainly not all, young people with ADHD may find literacy difficult. This may be due to difficulties with executive function. They may find it harder to focus while reading and writing, have difficulty organising their thoughts and find comprehension tasks more challenging.

- **Autism** – This can on occasion impact some areas of literacy. For example, some autistic students may find comprehension tasks difficult – in particular, when inferring information from a text. Some autistic students who may think more literally may also find understanding idioms and metaphors challenging.

- **Vision impairment or low vision** – Having a vision impairment may mean a young person needs more support in accessing the curriculum, including literacy. The Curriculum Framework for Children and Young People with Vision Impairment (CFVI) has been developed to ensure children with a vision impairment can access the curriculum. The framework is split into sections, including a section on literacy skills. Find out more on the Royal National Institute of Blind People (RNIB) website (see *Further Reading and Support*).

- **Global developmental delay (GDD)** – This means a young person may have taken longer than their peers to reach certain developmental milestones. Students with GDD can have literacy difficulties, in particular, with reading comprehension, organising written work and applying understanding to their written work. Some students with GDD also have SLCN which can impact their literacy skills.

- **Down's syndrome** – Some, but not all, students with Down's syndrome may find reading and writing more challenging. This may be due, in part, to difficulties with phonological awareness and word decoding.

- **Hyperlexia** – While young people with hyperlexia will have exceptional reading skills, they may need support with comprehension and verbal understanding.

- **Hearing loss/deafness** – Hearing loss/deafness can impact on a young person's literacy skills (particularly the acquisition of early literacy skills such as phonological awareness).

WHAT YOU MIGHT NOTICE

While many reading and writing difficulties may have been identified at primary school, as the National Literacy Trust's report (2024) explains, 'we cannot rely on primary schools to identify reading needs'. It's also worth noting that some reading and writing difficulties won't resolve in primary school and therefore students will still need support in secondary. There will also be some difficulties that will become apparent in secondary school (National Literacy Trust, 2024). It's therefore important to be aware of ways that students with reading and writing difficulties may present.

Young people with literacy difficulties may have challenges with (although not limited to) the following:

▶ **Behaviour** – It must be incredibly frustrating for some students with reading and/or writing difficulties in lessons. The vast majority of the curriculum is accessed this way and therefore, it's no surprise that students with literacy difficulties can sometimes become disillusioned in lessons. This may result in behaviour ranging from appearing uninterested or attempting to avoid literacy-based tasks to behaviour that disrupts the lessons.

▶ **Difficulties with speech, language and communication** – It's worth remembering that the students in your lessons who have SLCN may also have difficulties with reading and writing. Speech, language and communication skills are an integral part of literacy skills. I would recommend reading Chapter 1 alongside this chapter to see whether a student's difficulties in this area could also impact on their literacy skills.

▶ **Handwriting** – Students who have gross and/or fine motor skill difficulties (see Chapter 4) may find handwriting difficult. There are lots of ways you can support young people either as a parent/carer at home or teacher; read through the suggestions in Chapter 4 to help develop these skills alongside any external agency support the young person may have.

▶ **Fatigue during literacy tasks** – Students with difficulties with reading and/or writing are likely to be putting in significantly more effort into every lesson than their peers, in order to stay on track. Therefore, students with reading and/or writing difficulties may present with fatigue during literacy tasks. It could manifest as not having the same stamina as their peers when writing lengthy answers or appearing disengaged when reading longer passages. Be mindful not to presume a lack of motivation, but instead use your professional curiosity to see if literacy difficulties may be a barrier for their learning. It could also be due to muscle fatigue, either their core stabilising muscles needed to sit comfortably in their chair, or the muscles in their hands and fingers needed for writing. It would be worth reading

Chapter 4 alongside this chapter for support on gross and fine motor skill difficulties.

- **Difficulties with comprehension** – Reading proficiency includes the ability to understand and use the information they read to answer questions. However, some students may find this skill more difficult. This might be due to a limited vocabulary or accidentally skipping parts of the text while reading, which can happen with some students who have ADHD, for example. Young people who have difficulties with working memory or processing skills may also find comprehension challenging. Moreover, comprehension questions that require inference can be particularly difficult for students who think more literally, such as some autistic students or for those who have limited, prior background knowledge to draw upon.
- **Difficulties with reading fluency** – If a student has difficulty with reading fluency, they may struggle to read smoothly. For example, dyslexia can affect a student's ability to read fluently. Students with difficulties with reading fluency may feel self-conscious when reading texts out loud.

STRATEGIES

Here are some strategies for both school and home to help young people develop their reading and writing skills. If a student receives support from an external professional, ensure you are also implementing their suggestions of strategies.

IN THE CLASSROOM

These strategies are designed specifically for the classroom, suitable for both teachers and teaching assistants.

READING

- **Time** – Give students sufficient time to read texts and information on the board. To support students with reading difficulties who need to read large amounts of text during a lesson, you could explore providing them with the text before the lesson to allow them to prepare.
- **Use technology** – There are so many ways we can support students with reading difficulties using technology (see the *Resources* section). Technology doesn't just help a student right now in their lesson to access reading materials, it can also help them to

develop a toolkit of resources for when they are older and in the world of work.

- **Chunk text** – A page of continuous text can be incredibly difficult to read for many students with reading difficulties including dyslexia. A simple way to make text more accessible is to break it into smaller chunks. It may also be beneficial for some students to support these paragraphs with visuals.

- **Explore fonts, spacing, colours and sizes** – There's been a lot of research over the past few years on dyslexia-friendly fonts. There is some evidence that specific dyslexia fonts are no more beneficial than regular fonts (Kuster *et al*, 2018). However, it is evident that some fonts are easier to read than others, especially for dyslexic students. Therefore, it's a good idea to speak to the student and find out their font preferences. The British Dyslexia Association provides some excellent guidance on choice of fonts, sizes, letter spacing and colours (see their website for more information).

- **Ensure reading materials are accessible** – It goes without saying that if you're providing a student with some written text that is way above their reading age, to read as part of any lesson, they aren't going to be able to access it easily. One great place for testing the approximate reading age of materials is the 'Readability Test' on the Webfx website; you can also simplify text via the free website Rewordify.

COMPREHENSION

- **Assess and develop background knowledge and understanding** – Many comprehension-based activities rely to some extent on a student's prior knowledge and understanding. Having limited prior knowledge/understanding of a topic can therefore act as a barrier to learning. To support students with background understanding, use strategies such as group and class discussions and paired/group mind map activities. These mind maps can then be used as a visual support for comprehension work.

- **Notes/doodles in the margin** – A useful skill, to teach students when making sense of a text that they are reading, is to jot down notes or create doodles in the margin to support themselves. It can be a tricky skill to acquire and may need to be modelled for them, perhaps using a visualiser to show the whole class the sorts of things to note down in the margin and why.

- **No writing comprehension** – This is when students read a text but answer verbally without having to write down the answers.

This can be helpful for students with literacy difficulties as it enables them to demonstrate their understanding without the added difficulty of writing down their answers. It can also be used as a strategy to use before students need to write their ideas down, allowing them to verbally plan their answers first. You could also voice record students' answers to support them when writing.

- **Invent their questions** – One way to support the development of comprehension skills is to ask students to think of their own questions. For example, if they were reading a page of information in science on cells – they could go through the text and write down questions about it, designed for others to answer.

WRITING

- **Reduce unnecessary pressure** – While it's important and necessary to provide lots of opportunities to help develop students' writing skills across the curriculum, we must also be mindful of the cumulative effect on students with literacy difficulties of completing several written tasks throughout the day. Impacts include: fatigue (especially if they have motor difficulties), self-esteem (if finding every written task difficult) and disengagement. Therefore, I urge you to think about the desired outcome of all the tasks you're setting and question if each one definitely requires the student to record written answers or if one of the tasks could be completed in a different way. If students are demonstrating understanding verbally in some tasks, this can also have the added benefit of supporting their speech, language and communication skills.

- **Use technology** – One way to demonstrate understanding without having to write is to use technology (see *Resources* for more ideas). For example, we can use speech-to-text software to convert a student's spoken words into written text.

- **Paired writing** – Paired writing is when two students team up to plan, write, revise or edit a piece of written work together. This approach lets them support each other and learn new writing skills.

- **Mind map** – Teach students to plan their written work first, using a mind map of the key ideas and vocabulary to include.

- **Sentence starters** – Some students with literacy difficulties can find it difficult to start a written task. Providing students with suggestions of phrases to start their sentences can not only help them to get started on the task sooner but also improve the quality of their written answers.

▶ **Visual prompts** – Visual prompts can be very helpful for supporting students with literacy difficulties when writing. You may choose to provide a picture, for example, relating to the topic to stimulate ideas and provide context.

▶ **Model and/or provide structure** – Providing consistent support with structuring written work can be especially beneficial for students who struggle to organise their ideas and find a blank page daunting. To support this you could model on the board/visualiser how to structure written answers, or you could provide a writing frame (a template to help organise ideas) for written tasks.

SPELLING

▶ **Create their own subject-specific key word spelling book** – Explore whether students could create a key word spelling book in your lessons, recording subject-specific vocabulary with definitions. This not only helps students with the spelling and meaning of key words for your subject, but it helps them to keep up with the increased demands of subject-specific vocabulary in secondary school.

▶ **Mnemonics** – For some students, mnemonics can be a helpful way to remember how to spell key subject-specific words.

▶ **Spelling games** – There are lots of games, both online and offline, that students can play to help develop their spelling. You could choose certain key subject-specific vocabulary you're learning to be included in the game. Offline classroom games include hangman, word bingo and crosswords.

ACROSS THE SCHOOL

While teachers can use strategies in the classroom to support children with literacy difficulties, having a school-wide approach as well (led by the SENDCo and/or SLT) may enable more consistency. It's also worth noting that many strategies and whole-school approaches are likely to benefit all students and not just those with literacy difficulties.

▶ **Reading role models** – Promote staff as reading role models. To do this you could encourage members of teaching and non-teaching staff within the school to discuss and share with students what they are reading at the moment, their favourite books, as well as explaining when they are finding opportunities to read. You could use corridor displays to show which books members of staff are currently reading.

- **Whole-school literacy audit** – It could be beneficial to carry out a whole-school audit for literacy support, assessing the school's literacy practices, training and resources to pinpoint strengths and areas needing improvement. The aim is to ensure that all students, particularly those with SEND, receive the support necessary to develop strong literacy skills.

- **Opportunity to share good literacy skill development practice** – There will be members of staff in your school who are fantastic at supporting students with literacy difficulties within their lessons. Share this good practice. This could be through CPD, student voice, staff briefings and providing opportunities for staff to observe these strategies in action.

- **Identify and support early** – Assessing all students early in Year 7 to identify which students will need more support is vital to enable you to provide high-quality, targeted literacy interventions for students who are finding literacy more difficult.

- **Question silent reading at form time** – While reading in school should be encouraged, there is some evidence that silent reading isn't as beneficial as once thought. The Education Endowment Foundation (EEF) reports that the impacts of silent reading on student outcomes and motivation is inconsistent (Quigley & Coleman, 2019).

- **After-school/lunchtime clubs to promote reading** – If not already provided by your school, try introducing lunchtime or after-school clubs that help to promote and encourage reading, ensuring they are accessible for all abilities. This could include book clubs, for example.

- **Word of the day/week** – Include a word of the day/week in form times, on the school website or via the school newsletter to develop students' vocabulary.

- **Word games during form time** – Look at encouraging word games during form time, such as word bingo, hangman and scrabble. Different subject areas could take turns to provide subject-specific vocabulary to practise.

- **Literacy training for teachers specific to subject needs** – Different subjects will have varying needs in terms of literacy training. Ensuring any training provided meets each subjects' specific needs is key to its effectiveness.

- **No pens day** – The charity Speech and Language UK run a 'no pens day' campaign each year to encourage exactly that – a day of no pens! This is not only a novel and brilliant opportunity to develop speech, language and communication skills but it can also be beneficial for the self-esteem of students with writing difficulties – enabling them to demonstrate their understanding (all day!) in a different way. See their website for more information.

- **School ethos of 'vocab learners'** – As mentioned in Chapter 1, there are lots of ways you can do this including ensuring vocabulary development is developed across the curriculum (not just in English), vocabulary is taught explicitly, there's a culture of reading, a vocabulary-rich school environment and engagement with families on key vocabulary (this could be done through the school website/portal and newsletters).

- **Create a consistent approach to how vocabulary is introduced and taught across subjects** – The increased language demands of the secondary school curriculum mean that students have to learn a lot of new complex vocabulary in different subjects. Some of these words also have different meanings depending on the subject. Having a consistent approach to how new vocabulary is introduced and reinforced will help students with this.

- **Literacy student voice** – Don't presume we have all the answers; speak to students and collect 'student voice' on what strategies are working for them and what more we can do to help. Not only does this better inform our support, but it also gives students the agency and autonomy to speak up for themselves on what they need, which is a useful life skill to develop.

AT HOME

Young people don't just develop literacy skills at school and therefore the role of the young person's family is paramount. If you're a parent or carer reading this, these strategies might be helpful for supporting your child, but *you* have the expertise on your own child and their needs, so pick and choose which ones will work best. If you're a teacher/SENDCo, these could be strategies you share with the families of the students with literacy difficulties you support.

OPPORTUNITIES FOR LITERACY

- **Daily reading in free time** – Daily reading in free time isn't just for primary-aged children. Try to encourage your young person to continue to read in their free time. It may be that you need to be more flexible with what they read but be led by their interests.

- **Word puzzles** – Word puzzles, such as crosswords, are brilliant for supporting young people's literacy skills. Set challenges together as a family to complete them. The Simply Daily Puzzles website provides new simple crosswords free every day.

- **Subtitles** – Setting your TV and any tablets to have subtitles on as a default is a great way of encouraging passive reading while watching films and programmes, so much so there's a whole campaign about subtitles – find out more at the Turn on the Subtitles website.

- **Everyday tasks** – It can be difficult to find opportunities for young people to read and write at home without being met with frustration. Try short but frequent tasks, such as helping you to jot down items on a shopping list or writing a thank you card. Or reading a recipe to you while you bake a cake, or reading out instructions from an instruction booklet for something you're building or fixing. You may find that anything that is a genuine task and not something you are asking them to do as 'extra homework' is better received.

- **Gaming that involves reading** – The vast majority of games that young people play on a gaming console require some reading (and often typing if playing with others).

SUPPORTING LITERACY SKILLS

- **Reading role model** – Young people are still influenced by the adults around them. If they see us reading and writing it may help to encourage them to try to do the same. Ensure young people in your care see you read and write regularly. Being honest with them if you find literacy challenging can be incredibly powerful, especially if you explain the strategies you use to support yourself with reading and writing.

- **Visits to the library** – Visiting the library can be beneficial for young students with literacy difficulties for many reasons. Firstly, they provide a wide range of books enabling young people to find books suitable for their reading level that are also age-appropriate (the librarians will be able to support with this). They also often provide access to audiobooks and e-books, making reading more accessible. And the general environment of a library is supportive, quiet and calm – providing young people with a space that isn't overstimulating for reading (and studying). I can vouch for this having written part of this book in my local library! There are also opportunities for young people to get involved with volunteering at local libraries, for example, during the summer, 'reading challenges' that are often run by teenage volunteers alongside library staff for younger children.

- **Audiobooks** – Although it may seem counterintuitive, audiobooks can significantly enhance a young person's reading skills. They provide numerous benefits, such as offering an accessible entry point for students who struggle with reading. Audiobooks allow these students to enjoy captivating stories that they might not have been able to experience through traditional reading.

- **Technology** – We have incredible technology today that makes literacy more accessible, so let's embrace it! How often do you write sentences with a pen or pencil? I hardly ever do! I bet this generation of young people will use pens and pencils even less frequently as adults. Allowing a young person who struggles with writing to use a word processor for writing not only removes current barriers to learning but also prepares them for how they will access literacy in the future. (For more examples of technology that can support literacy skills, see the *Resources* section of this chapter.)

- **Support them with subject-specific vocabulary** – They will be learning lots of new words in all their subjects in school. Speak to their teachers/SENDCo to ask to be sent new vocabulary that they can practise together at home.

RESOURCES

INTERVENTIONS AND PROGRAMMES

- **Lexia® PowerUp Literacy®** – For secondary-aged students who do not yet have the essential academic vocabulary, reading and comprehension skills needed to fully access the curriculum.

- **DocsPlus** – DocsPlus is a writing tool designed to support secondary school students with reading difficulties by providing tools for planning, drafting and proofing their work. DocsPlus offers features like word prediction, writing frames and curriculum vocabulary banks to boost writing confidence and success. A full review can be found on my website The SEN Resources Blog.

- **Words for All** – A professional development framework that collaborates with schools and trusts to enhance reading culture, boost confidence and improve students' academic outcomes.

- **Read Write Inc. (RWI) Fresh Start programme** – The RWI Fresh Start programme, by Ruth Miskin Literacy, is a systematic synthetic phonics intervention for older students (generally aged 9–13 and up) who find reading difficult. It aims to enhance reading accuracy, fluency and stamina, with 25-minute, daily sessions.

- **The Reading and Language Intervention for Children with Down's syndrome (RLI)** – RLI is a teaching programme created to develop reading and language skills for students with Down's syndrome. It involves daily one-to-one intervention sessions to supplement regular teaching.

- **IDL Literacy Software** – Intervention software used in many secondary schools to support students with dyslexia and other SEND that may impact literacy skills. It helps students to increase their reading and spelling ages. While designed as an intervention software, it can also be used school-wide as a literacy software solution.

- **Talk for Writing** – Talk for Writing approach started in the primary sector but is now also used in secondary schools. It is a flexible teaching method that enhances student understanding and expression. It moves from imitation to innovation and then to independent application. This approach develops reading, writing and speaking skills and can be used across the curriculum.

- **Dyslexia Gold** – Online programmes to teach eye control, phonological awareness, phonics and vocabulary. Suitable for some students in Key Stage 3 (and primary), with or without a dyslexia diagnosis.

- **Accelerated Reader** – This is a web-based programme that aims to encourage independent reading and reading for pleasure. It assesses students to provide teachers with students' reading ages (flagging which students may need further support). It also uses their reading ages and their interests (found during the assessments) to suggest suitable books for them to read, and provides quizzes to complete after each book. The Education Endowment Fund (EEF) (2015) says that 'Accelerated Reader appears to be effective for weaker readers as a catch-up intervention at the start of secondary school.' But it is worth noting that they also report that 'Pupils at very low levels of reading may not be independent readers and would need initial support from teacher to start reading books.'

OTHER RESOURCES

▶ **Text-to-speech apps** – These apps can read aloud text that appears on paper or a screen.

▶ **Reading pens** – A portable tool that students can use on their own to aid their reading. By swiping it over text (including exam papers), it reads the words aloud. Headphones can be connected to ensure privacy and enable them to be discrete.

▶ **E-readers** – An electronic book reader, like a Kindle, can be an incredibly useful tool for students with literacy difficulties. They can adjust the font, font size, text colour, background colour and more, to make reading easier. Additionally, these devices often allow users to look up word definitions, highlight text and even have the content read aloud.

▶ **Audiobooks** – Not only do these offer a 'way in' to access more exciting stories for students with reading difficulties but they can make literacy tasks that are based on a book more accessible. Listening to an audio version of a text/book enables students to listen, pause and rewind, allowing them to focus on the content of the story instead of how to read the words.

▶ **Sticky notes** – A budget-friendly resource for organising ideas and planning written work, as well as jotting down questions, key points and questions during reading.

▶ **Highlighters** – Highlighter pens are a fantastically useful tool for organisation. Students can use them to mark key points in a text before answering questions about it. Teaching students to use highlighter pens effectively is valuable, as this skill can be beneficial for them even as adults.

▶ **Word processor** – As mentioned earlier, this generation of young people is unlikely to use pencils and pens regularly as adults due to advancing technology. Therefore, allowing a student who struggles to write with a pencil to use a word processor is a great idea. It not only helps them to access the curriculum now but also allows them to practise typing skills, preparing them for adulthood and work.

▶ **Motor skill resources** – See Chapter 4 for a list of resources that can help students with their motor skills.

▶ **Spelling and grammar check** – Spelling and grammar checks on word processors can be helpful for students to learn how to spell and improve their sentences. Grammarly is a particularly useful example as it enables students to improve their writing by checking for grammar, spelling, punctuation and style errors as they go along.

▶ **Read&Write** – Developed by Everway, Read&Write is a literacy support tool designed to support students with reading text aloud, understanding unfamiliar words, researching assignments and proofreading written work.

FURTHER READING AND SUPPORT

Websites

And Next Comes L: 'Your Go-to resource for hyperlexia' www.andnextcomesl.com

British Dyslexia Association www.bdadyslexia.org.uk

Choosing a phonics teaching programme www.gov.uk/government/publications/choosing-a-phonics-teaching-programme/list-of-phonics-teaching-programmes

Curriculum Framework for Children and Young people with Vision Impairment (CFVI) www.rnib.org.uk/professionals/health-social-care-education-professionals/education-professionals/curriculum-framework-for-children-and-young-people-with-vision-impairment

DocsPlus www.cricksoft.com/docsplus

'Hyperlexia' by CHAT www.chatwithus.org/conditions/hyperlexia

Irlen Institute www.irlen.com

Nessy www.nessy.com/en-gb

Rewordify https://rewordify.com/

Spellzone www.spellzone.com

The Communication Trust website www.slcframework.org.uk and www.fis.cityoflondon.gov.uk/asset-library/tct-univspeak-11-18.pdf

Webfx 'Readability Test' www.webfx.com/tools/read-able

Books

All About Dyslexia: A Practical Guide for Secondary Teachers by Louise Selby

Dyslexia Is My Superpower (Most of the Time) by Margaret Rooke

Literacy Learning Journeys: An Educator's Guide to Dyslexia ages 0–18 by Dr Helen Ross

The Spelling Rulebook by SEN Marketing

CHAPTER 3
NUMERACY SKILLS

CASE STUDY

SARAH JOHNSON, AN EXPERIENCED TEACHER, AUTHOR AND EDUCATION CONSULTANT, SHARES HER EXPERIENCES OF LIVING WITH UNDIAGNOSED DYSCALCULIA DURING SECONDARY SCHOOL, REFLECTING ON THE CONFUSION AND ANXIETY SHE FELT AROUND MATHS AND THE SUPPORT SHE WISHES HAD BEEN AVAILABLE TO HELP HER UNDERSTAND HER LEARNING NEEDS.

When I was in primary school, I remember being made to do extra numeracy lessons because I couldn't tell the time. If you ask me now to do the same, well I still can't. I'm an educated woman with a master's degree, but if you ask me to look at a traditional clock face and tell you the time, I'll struggle. It doesn't matter how many extra maths lessons or worksheets I was given, it never seemed to make much of a difference.

I remember feeling confused and even resentful about why I was made to spend so much extra time on a subject I disliked. I would have much rather been doing English, art, or, frankly, anything else. I was also separated from my friends to be in a class for younger children. It wasn't great for my self-esteem. Maths was a constant source of frustration, and over time affected my confidence. I compared myself to my friends and classmates, and it was hard not to feel inadequate. They seemed to pick up maths so easily, while I struggled to understand even the basics. To this day, I still don't know my times tables, and numbers often get muddled in my mind. When I try and copy or write them down, I can only keep two numbers in my head.

When I was younger, remembering phone numbers was a necessity. You had to either memorise them or copy them down carefully as you dialled them into a handset. For me, it was incredibly difficult. I'd misremember or mix up the numbers almost every time. After several failed attempts, frustration would set in, and more often than not, I would just give up. These were small but frequent reminders that something about numbers simply didn't 'click' for me the way it seemed to for others.

It wasn't until much later, when I was at university, that I was diagnosed with dyscalculia. Suddenly, so much about my maths lessons made sense. It wasn't that I wasn't paying attention or wasn't trying hard enough. It was that my brain processed numbers differently. They didn't stay still on the page; it was as if they were dancing and making the patterns that others saw hard for me to see.

Reflecting back, I realise that although there were attempts to help me when I was younger, they weren't particularly effective. I was given extra lessons and more worksheets, but what I really needed was something else, what we'd now call adaptive teaching. I needed more scaffolding, hands-on materials like manipulatives and more time to process. I needed someone to understand that trying harder wasn't the issue; I needed to try differently.

Being diagnosed didn't make the difficulties disappear, but it gave me understanding and the language to explain my experiences. Dyscalculia still affects me daily, with things like telling the time, working out differences in world time zones and knowing how to travel from one place to another within a set time, but now I have strategies to accommodate this. I use digital clocks, calculators, apps and reminders. I screenshot journey plans and continually refer back to those plans to make sure I'm on the right track!

Most importantly, I know that my difficulties with numbers, reading maps (thank you sat navs!), getting from A to B, do not equate to my intelligence but are just an idiosyncratic part of how my brain works.

OVERVIEW OF NEEDS

If you've picked up this book hoping for a chapter on how to teach trigonometry, algebra, or those pesky simultaneous equations to secondary-aged students, then I'm very sorry to disappoint, but this chapter, and perhaps this entire book, might not be for you.

WHAT DO WE MEAN BY NUMERACY SKILLS?

When we read the phrase 'numeracy difficulties', we might picture a student in a maths classroom struggling to make sense of a tricky calculation or to follow along with a complex equation. It's a familiar image, and one that can lead us to mistakenly believe these challenges are limited to maths lessons, neatly contained by the classroom door and easily forgotten when the bell rings.

But, as Sarah Johnson so insightfully illustrated in her case study, the reality is far wider reaching. Difficulties with numeracy ripple through many aspects of a young person's life, often (to an onlooker) in quiet, unnoticed ways. In school, they may show up in science when interpreting graphs or measuring quantities, in geography while analysing data and reading maps, or in history through sequencing events or navigating timelines. Beyond the classroom, numeracy challenges surface in everyday tasks: reading a bus timetable, judging when to leave the house to arrive on time, splitting a bill with friends or working out fair teams for a football match.

Even though this chapter sits early in the book, I'll admit it was the last chapter I wrote, and the one I avoided writing the longest. Not because I think it's unimportant, but precisely because it's *so* important. And because, while 'on paper' I'm good at maths, I've never particularly felt confident with number-based tasks, and I worried I wasn't the right person to be writing about them. But my opinion changed after a conversation with someone who pointed out that the best people to support children with numeracy aren't always the ones who find maths easy – the ones who just 'get it' and haven't had to work at it. But instead, it's the ones who understand what it's like when numbers don't make sense, who get anxious when faced with a number-based task and who know how it feels to feel stuck. And because of that, they're the ones who can offer the most useful support, the workarounds, the strategies and the understanding. That really stayed with me, and gave me the confidence to write this chapter as honestly and practically as I could.

Because at its heart, numeracy is not just about solving sums. It's about applying number understanding in everyday situations, with enough confidence to make decisions, solve problems and feel in control. These are the foundational skills that help young people access the wider curriculum and, even more importantly, gain the independence they need to navigate day-to-day life.

That's why this chapter isn't about teaching the secondary maths curriculum. It's not a lesson plan or a step-by-step guide to algebra for students with SEND. Instead, it's about recognising when and where numeracy difficulties appear, across school, home and everyday life, and exploring what we can do to support them. It's about practical changes, strategies and the right resources to help every young person feel more confident and able when faced with numbers.

WHY ARE NUMERACY SKILLS IMPORTANT?

Like me, many of you may remember sitting in a secondary classroom, confused by a difficult maths problem, reaching for the calculator... only to be told by the teacher (again!): 'Try it without the calculator; you won't always have a calculator in your pocket.' Looking back, it was probably said to encourage independence and determination. But fast forward to today's digital age, and most of us do, thanks to smartphones, actually carry a calculator (along with a whole computer) every day in our pocket!

But jokes aside, despite our access to technology to support us with maths (which is brilliant), there is still a strong argument that it can only support and not replace the deeper understanding we get from building strong numeracy skills. Numeracy skills that are imperative, as we've explained, for young people's everyday life. We need to strike the very delicate balance of helping young people to develop a useful toolkit of strategies using technology to support their numeracy skills, while also continuing to look at different ways to help develop their numeracy skills.

Like we discussed in the chapter on literacy skills (Chapter 2), difficulties with numeracy have wide-reaching implications, especially for secondary-aged students. These range from challenges in accessing other aspects of the curriculum to low self-esteem, sometimes impacting on behaviour and engagement in school.

As students grow older, numeracy becomes central to financial literacy, a skillset that is increasingly essential. Teenagers will start making decisions that have real financial consequences. They may open bank accounts, manage wages from weekend jobs, or sign up for phone contracts. Soon they'll be faced with other, perhaps more complex financial situations, maybe navigating student loans, comparing rent prices, understanding pension contributions or working out interest on a credit card. Without numeracy skills, these decisions become much harder to understand, and mistakes can be costly and difficult to undo. *The Skills for Life Survey* (2012) found that nearly half of England's working-age adult population had numeracy levels no greater than primary-aged children (Department for Business, Innovation and Skills, 2012). A statistic that should not just prompt concern around numeracy skills in school, but on how we are supporting adults with financial independence.

Research also tells us that people with difficulties with numeracy are also linked to unemployment (National Numeracy, 2014), with the more recent National Numeracy Strategy (2025–28) reiterating that poor numeracy contributes to problems including employability and limits to career choices (National Numeracy, 2024). Again, this prompts us into thinking about how we are supporting numeracy skills across the board for secondary-aged young people.

WHO MIGHT NEED FURTHER SUPPORT WITH THEIR NUMERACY SKILLS?

There is a whole range of SEND that may affect a young person's numeracy skills. I stress 'may' as we must remember that all young people are unique and are certainly not defined by a SEND, and as such, they will have their own individual strengths and challenges.

Generally speaking, if you have students in your class with (but not limited to) the specific SENDs listed below, or your own child has one of these special educational needs or disabilities, then they may have difficulties with some areas of numeracy.

- **Dyscalculia** – Dyscalculia is a lifelong specific learning difficulty that affects around six per cent of the population, with an equal prevalence among boys and girls (BDA, n.d). In a typical classroom of 30 students this means that one or two children may be affected. It is worth noting that in March 2025, the SpLD Assessment Standards Committee (SASC) developed a new definition of dyscalculia. They describe it as a 'persistent difficulty with numerical magnitude processing and understanding that presents in age-related difficulties with naming, ordering and comparing physical qualities and numbers, estimating and place value' (SASC, 2025). Because of its impacts on a young person's ability to understand and work with numerical values and quantities, it can make everyday maths and number-based tasks particularly challenging.

- **Maths anxiety** – Maths anxiety is not simply a case of being 'worried about maths'; it's much more than that. Young people experiencing maths anxiety may show both psychological and physiological symptoms. These can include an increased heart rate or stomach ache/nausea when faced with mathematical tasks. Some may withdraw from learning altogether, avoiding further engagement with maths, while others might experience a mental block during specific activities. Children with dyscalculia often experience maths anxiety too. It's important to recognise that maths anxiety isn't exclusive to those who struggle with maths academically. In fact, a study by Carey *et al.* (2019) found that 'the vast majority (77 per cent) of children with high maths anxiety had typical or above-typical maths performance'.

- **Dyslexia** – It's a common misconception that dyslexia only affects reading and writing. In reality, dyslexia can also impact areas such as working memory, processing speed and sequencing, all of which play a vital role in mathematical thinking. As a result, some children with dyslexia may find aspects of numeracy more challenging, particularly when tasks involve multi-step procedures or require holding information in mind. Word-heavy maths problems can also present additional barriers due to the literacy demands involved. Importantly, the British Dyslexia Association (BDA, n.d) highlights that around 60 per cent of individuals with dyslexia also experience difficulties with maths, a reminder that support strategies should consider both literacy and numeracy needs together.

Other types of SEND linked to numeracy skills difficulties include:

- ADHD
- developmental delay
- Down's syndrome
- Williams syndrome
- Fragile X Syndrome (FXS)/Global Development Delay (GDD)
- Foetal Alcohol Syndrome (FAS).

WHAT YOU MIGHT NOTICE

For some students in secondary school, difficulties with numeracy may not always be immediately obvious, but they can have a significant impact on confidence, participation and progress.

MATHS LESSON SPECIFIC CHALLENGES

Mathematical concepts become more and more complex in secondary school and you may observe students presenting in the following ways as a result:

- avoiding activities that involve calculations, even if they're informal (e.g. maths-based games or quizzes)
- relying heavily on guesswork or estimations without using formal methods
- appearing withdrawn or disengaged in maths lessons, keeping quiet and not answering questions
- copying peers' work instead of attempting tasks independently
- hesitating to share answers during class feedback, or frequently crossing them out
- still using fingers or other counting aids when expected to calculate mentally
- needing additional time and or visual representations to process instructions and complete numeracy-based activities.

CROSS-CURRICULAR CHALLENGES IN SECONDARY SUBJECTS

As we've discussed, numeracy difficulties don't just affect maths; they can seep into other subjects where number concepts or mathematical thinking are essential, therefore, you may notice difficulties in any subject that involves numeracy skills, including (but definitely not limited to) these examples:

- **Science** – Students may find it hard to interpret data in tables, manipulate formulas, use correct units in experiments, or measure accurately (e.g. using a thermometer or measuring cylinder).

- **Design and technology** – Misjudging measurements in design work or using incorrect scaling might impact the accuracy of their final products. Budgeting in food technology tasks (e.g. working out the cost per portion) may also prove difficult.

- **History** – Understanding dates, timelines, calculating durations between historical events, or grasping numerical data (e.g. population growth) can be problematic.

- **Geography** – Skills like interpreting maps with a scale, reading charts and graphs and managing data in fieldwork all rely heavily on a solid numerical understanding.

- **PE** – Keeping score in competitive games, timing peers, or calculating performance statistics (e.g. time improvements, distance covered) may be difficult.

- **ICT** – Creating formulae in spreadsheets, coding and more can all pose challenges.

SCHOOL LIFE, LIFE SKILLS AND INDEPENDENCE

As secondary students grow older, numeracy challenges begin to affect wider aspects of school and life, particularly around independence, planning and preparation for adulthood. You may see that they find some of the following difficult:

- **Time and organisation skills** – Difficulties telling the time using an analogue clock, challenges estimating how long tasks will take (having a 'sense' of time), managing revision and revision schedules and interpreting time-based school timetables. Potentially these can lead to lateness and missed deadlines.

- **Self-esteem** – Students may avoid situations that involve numbers, leading to reduced participation and low self-esteem.

- **Real-life financial skills** – Tasks that involve using money (paying by cash or card), planning budgets for trips, calculating mobile phone costs or comparing wages and student finance options can be daunting without good numeracy foundations.

- **Directions** – May have confusion with left and right and difficulties following a map/directions.

STRATEGIES

Here are some strategies for both school and home to help young people develop their reading and writing skills. If a student receives support from an external professional, ensure you are also implementing their suggestions of strategies. Key to these strategies is the understanding that, as Sarah explained in the case study, it's not about trying harder but trying *differently*.

IN THE CLASSROOM

These strategies are designed specifically for the classroom, suitable for both teachers and teaching assistants.

- **Framing** – I think this one can be a really delicate balance. By the time a young person is in secondary school, their views around their abilities and confidence in numeracy may be quite well established. But it's our role to still try to frame numeracy-related tasks across the school positively to avoid reinforcing any negative attitudes. I do give a caveat with this though, that we mustn't be 'too positive'. It is important that we still recognise and do not underplay their real difficulties and lack of confidence in this area.

- **Praise effort** – Numeracy activities can be frustrating across school, because there are often only right or wrong answers. Praising effort not just accuracy can be really helpful for self-esteem, creating an environment where students feel safe to take risks without fear of getting it wrong.

- **Repetition** – Some young people may benefit from more repetition when it comes to instructions for numeracy activities and also of the numeracy-based tasks themselves. You can support by integrating quick recap tasks and revisiting key ideas regularly to support memory and reduce anxiety.

- **Prioritise understanding over memorisation** – The key to solid numeracy skills is often understanding, not remembering. If this means revisiting Key Stage 2 foundations when necessary, do this and build up from there. Meeting learners where they are at, not where they *should* be, is such an important part of adaptive and inclusive teaching practice.

- **Be mindful of language** – There's a lot of complex language involved around maths and numeracy. Choosing consistent vocabulary (e.g. sticking with 'subtract' instead of switching between 'minus' and 'take away') can be helpful, as is supporting students with SLCN using visuals. Sharing key numeracy vocabulary with parents/carers can be helpful to ensure consistency in language.

- **Provide real-life context** – Making numeracy tasks relevant can help to make it more engaging and worthwhile for young people who are finding it difficult. This might be linking it to day-to-day real-life uses, e.g, paying for items, using a bus timetable or budgeting.

- **Don't rule out concrete and visual supports** – manipulatives and images don't need to stay in primary school, again, we are meeting young people where they are at, not where we think they should be. For some young people, having concrete and visual supports will be needed and helpful (see *Resources*).

ACROSS THE SCHOOL

While teachers can use strategies in the classroom to support children with numeracy difficulties, having a school-wide approach as well (led by the SENDCo and/or SLT) may enable more consistency. It's also worth noting that many strategies and whole-school approaches are likely to benefit all students and not just those with numeracy difficulties (as well as those young people with numeracy difficulties who have not been identified).

- **Embed opportunities to develop numeracy skills and ensure consistent approaches to teaching across departments and subjects** – As we've discussed, numeracy doesn't just belong in the maths classroom; it appears across a wide range of subjects including science, geography, history and more. Consistency in how numeracy is taught and supported throughout the curriculum is essential to help students make meaningful connections and build confidence. Part of this will be promoting consistent language and representations to avoid confusing students with different terminology or strategies.

- **Develop staff confidence in numeracy across the curriculum** – It's important to ensure staff across all subjects feel confident and able to support numeracy difficulties within their subject area. This might be through internal or external professional development and sharing of good practice across the school.

▶ **Raise the profile of numeracy** – This could be achieved through initiatives like competitions, school trips, quizzes, themed celebrations, or learning about influential mathematicians, and careers that rely on numeracy. While we must be careful to remember that promoting a love of maths won't eliminate challenges young people face, especially those linked to SEND, for example, dyscalculia or maths anxiety, it can make numeracy feel less intimidating, foster engagement and help to build awareness and understanding of specific needs.

AT HOME

Young people don't just develop and practise numeracy skills at school and therefore the role of the young person's family is paramount. If you're a parent or carer reading this, these strategies might be helpful for supporting your child, but *you* have the expertise on your own child and their needs, so pick and choose which ones will work best. If you're a teacher/SENDCo, these could be strategies you share with the families of the students with numeracy difficulties you support.

Supporting young people to build confidence with numeracy can be done by actively trying to include numeracy-based tasks as part of everyday situations. Not only does this mean it feels less pressurised and more subtle, but it also gives purpose to practising these skills, as they aren't just practising 'for the sake of it' but to help them as part of life skills and to become more independent.

Ways families can do this include:

▶ **Providing opportunities to manage money (safely)** – This could be letting them handle budgeting for shopping, comparing mobile phone plans, or if they are old enough for a part-time job, reviewing wages and payslips. And safety should be prioritised here, as this should be done with the reassurance that you're still there to support and check that any errors made don't become costly while they are developing financial literacy skills.

▶ **Talking about time** – Time awareness can be a really tricky skill to develop. Families can help by talking about durations (journey lengths, etc.), deadlines and plans using clocks, calendars or planners to develop time awareness. There are lots of time management apps on phones that can help, as well as the basic functions on phones such as reminders, calendar notifications and alarms.

- **Reinforcing maths language in everyday life** – Try to use maths language at home during everyday tasks, to normalise and reinforce its meaning. It also helps them to make links to real life and prevent maths concepts from being abstract.
- **Using technology to build a toolkit** – Work together to try out apps and other technology to develop a personalised toolkit of resources/strategies that they can use to navigate numeracy-based activities during everyday life.

RESOURCES

Numeracy resources aren't just for younger children; they're valuable tools for learners of all ages. For secondary students, especially those who may have missed key foundations earlier on or who have additional learning needs, these resources can support access to more complex content and help to rebuild confidence. Reintroducing familiar resources from earlier stages can create continuity, while layering in new conceptual understanding.

Crucially, these tools aren't just for demonstration. When students can see, touch and manipulate maths themselves, it becomes more concrete, less abstract and easier to make sense of. As Sarah explained in her case study, hands-on materials like manipulatives can be really helpful. Many of the items below are multisensory, meaning they use more than one sense. This can help support retention and make maths more accessible – particularly for students with dyscalculia or dyslexia.

- **Graph paper** – A simple but powerful tool to help students organise numbers, align equations and reduce confusion – particularly helpful sometimes for young people who struggle with place value.
- **Numicon shapes** – Often considered more for early years at primary school, but Numicon can be incredibly effective at secondary too.
- **2D and 3D shape models** – Physical models bring geometry and spatial reasoning to life: great for learners who need to feel shape properties or build their understanding through handling real objects.

- **Magformers and nets** – Constructing with magnetic shapes supports spatial awareness, symmetry and scale; it turns abstract nets into meaningful, memorable models.

- **Dominoes** – Games are underrated in numeracy support but examples such as dominoes can be fantastic for supporting numeracy skills through age-appropriate play. Dominoes, in particular, can be useful for young people who have difficulties around subitising, for example (but not limited to), those with dyscalculia.

- **Dienes blocks** – Still relevant beyond primary school, they help secondary students to revisit place value, decimals and build a strong understanding of base-ten structure.

- **Interlocking cubes** – Hands on and flexible, ideal for bar charts, area modelling or comparing fractions in a visual, active way.

- **Real coins** – Essential for practical maths and financial literacy, great for hands-on tactile teaching of budgeting, change and everyday value.

- **Cuisenaire rods** – A go-to for visualising fractions and proportions.

- **Geoboards** – Excellent for shape construction and angle measurement, there are virtual versions too if physical boards aren't available.

- *Numberblocks* – Although this TV programme has been developed for younger children, some older students with more complex needs benefit hugely from its clear, engaging visuals and repetitive structure.

- **Apps** – I won't recommend individual apps here, as technology is so fast paced that they may well be out of date by the time you're reading this. But there are many apps that can help with a whole host of numeracy-based tasks to support young people; a simple search on a smartphone or tablet will come up with plenty of choice.

Further Reading and Support

Websites

Awareness of Developmental Dyscalculia and Mathematical Difficulties toolkit by UCL:

www.ucl.ac.uk/ioe/departments-and-centres/psychology-and-human-development/research/child-development-and-learning-difficulties-lab/awareness-developmental-dyscalculia-and-mathematical-difficulties-toolkit-add

Dyscalculia Network www.dyscalculianetwork.com

Books

100 Ideas for Secondary Teachers: Supporting Students with Numeracy Difficulties by Patricia Babtie and Sue Dillon

Maths Anxiety: Solving the Equation by Heidi Kirkland and Tom Hunt

Maths Learning Difficulties, Dyslexia and Dyscalculia: Second Edition by Steve Chinn

CHAPTER 4

MOTOR SKILLS

CASE STUDY

KAT CAUCHI, A COMMUNITY ENGAGEMENT MANAGER, EDUCATION MAGAZINE EDITOR AND FORMER PRIMARY SCHOOL TEACHER, SHARES HER EXPERIENCES OF DEVELOPMENTAL COORDINATION DISORDER (DCD) AT SECONDARY SCHOOL.

When I was around four or five years old I was diagnosed with DCD/dyspraxia. While each person's experience of this condition is different, the main areas of impact for me are on my motor skills and coordination. This has improved significantly in my adulthood but I do still find that writing or typing for long periods of time can cause me pain or discomfort. Since DCD does impact my motor skills and coordination, I can get tired easily from physical activity. This made motivation for exercise very difficult for me until I was able to find a form that I really enjoyed.

When I was at secondary school, other than extra time in exams (that I never found I needed), I didn't have any additional support. This differed from my primary school experience where I was, for example, given typing lessons and supported with fine and gross motor skill development.

I honestly think no one in my school really understood my condition due to lack of training and awareness. This isn't to say that teachers in my school were uncaring; I think they just hadn't got the tools to support them in order to be able to support me.

It's difficult to say exactly what could have helped me in school, particularly as I didn't want to feel 'different' to anyone else; I liked to be independent and defy expectations. For example, when I was very young, doctors said I may not be able to handwrite but I continued to work on it until I could write as much and, in some cases, more than my peers. I also managed very well at secondary school so this may have also been a factor in not receiving support. My condition was almost 'hidden', as it were.

But there are a few things that come to mind that would have been beneficial for me in secondary school; firstly, my teachers having more awareness of my condition and how it could impact me. Secondly, a conversation about what I wanted, what might help me, what was I finding difficult, etc. That communication was lacking and would have helped me to feel more valued and supported in school. Thirdly, PE was a bit of a nightmare for me. I found it hard, it was tiring, I wasn't very good at sports and so I was usually one of the last to get picked in teams. I think if I had been offered support outside of class to build up strength and coordination, that could have really helped. Also, if teachers stopped letting 'team captains' always pick their teammates, that would have boosted my self-esteem!

So all in all, I would sum it up to three things really: understanding, communication and empathy.

OVERVIEW OF NEEDS

Before we leap into this chapter on motor skills, I think it's essential to explain the two different types of motor skills we are covering.

WHAT DO WE MEAN BY MOTOR SKILLS?

- **Fine motor** – These skills focus on the use and control of the small muscles in someone's hands, wrists, fingers, toes, tongue, lips and so on, to perform precise or 'fine' movements. Fine motor skills are essential for various tasks, ranging from tying shoe laces to texting to using utensils at meals. Because of this, they are crucial for teenagers to achieve greater independence and to confidently navigate everyday activities.

- **Gross motor** – These skills involve using their larger, core-stabilising muscles. Young people need these muscles to walk, run, climb and jump. Just like fine motor skills, these are crucial for gaining independence. Adolescents rely on these skills for activities such as walking up and down stairs safely, carrying items and maintaining good posture while sitting at a desk for school work.

While fine and gross motor skill development is often at the forefront of primary school teachers' minds in reception when supporting children to learn to write, unless you're a PE teacher or a SENDCo, it's unlikely to be an area that you've been given much training in, despite the fact that motor difficulties will affect students in most of your lessons. For example, one SEND that impacts motor skills is Developmental Coordination Disorder (DCD), which is also referred to as dyspraxia, and this affects between five to six per cent of school-aged students (Khairati et al., 2023): at least one student in a class of 30.

NOT JUST ABOUT MUSCLE DEVELOPMENT

It's crucial to develop and support young people's motor skills, whether for core stability, essential to gross motor control, or fine motor control requiring dexterity in fingers and toes. However, motor skills encompass far more than just muscle development. If only it were that straightforward! Our bodies are intricate systems. For a young person to successfully write neatly, ride their bike with their friends or carry some science equipment across the science lab, they need more than just muscle power. They must be able to move in a coordinated manner and handle objects with dexterity. To achieve this, the following are also involved:

- **Motor planning skills** – This enables students to sequence and organise the steps to take when moving parts of their body.

- **Bilateral integration/coordination** – This refers to using both sides of the body in harmony, such as when using both hands together.

- **Crossing the midline** – This involves crossing an imaginary line dividing the left and right sides of the body with their arms or legs to perform tasks. Effective crossing of the midline requires communication between both sides of the brain, which also enhances skills like critical thinking.
- **Sensory processing** – This is the ability to interpret and respond to sensory information from all their senses. (See Chapter 5 for more information.)

LINK BETWEEN SENSORY INPUT AND MOTOR SKILLS

When we think about the senses, we often recall the five senses we learned about in school: touch, sight, hearing, smell and taste. However, it's a bit more complex than that. These are primarily our external senses, but we also receive sensory messages from within our bodies. These internal sensory inputs include, but aren't limited to:

- **Interoception** – Sensory feedback from internal organs and hormones. Examples include the urge to use the toilet, experiencing stomach aches, or feeling hungry or thirsty.
- **Proprioception** – Awareness of the position and movement of our body parts in space. For instance, this is how we know where our arms and legs are even with our eyes closed (try it!).
- **Balance (vestibular input)** – This sense helps us to maintain balance even while moving. When we move our heads, the fluid in our inner ears also moves and our vestibular system helps us to stay balanced by sensing these movements.

So how do these relate to motor skills activities? In simple terms, sensory input is essential for coordinating movements. For example, imagine a young person writing down a word that a teacher has written on the board. To do this, they need to:

- **Look** at the letters being written on the board and read the words being formed.
- **Know** where their hand and pencil are on the paper and move their hand in a coordinated way to form the letters (vision, touch, proprioception, vestibular).
- **Think** about how hard they are pressing the pen onto the paper (touch input) to apply the correct amount of pressure for writing.

Additionally, they need to ignore background noises or other visual and tactile distractions, while their interoception sense might be signalling hunger or other internal sensations.

FINE MOTOR SKILLS

WHY ARE THEY IMPORTANT?

Supporting young people with fine motor skill difficulties at school as a teacher or at home as a parent is really important for many reasons.

First and foremost, fine motor skills help young people to be independent. They enable them to complete school work themselves, text their peers after school and learn to be successful with life skills that they will need in adulthood, such as preparing simple meals, helping with laundry and basic DIY. They are also needed for self-care tasks, such as brushing their teeth and using deodorant.

Fine motor skill difficulties can also impact academic success, self-esteem and mental health. Research shows that children with DCD, for example, are less likely than their peers to achieve five or more GCSEs at grades 9–4 (previously A*–C) (Harrowell et al., 2018). And students diagnosed with DCD in childhood were 'twice as likely as their peers to have mental health problems in their late teens' (Harrowell et al., 2017).

WHO MIGHT NEED FURTHER SUPPORT WITH FINE MOTOR SKILLS?

Generally speaking, if you have students in your class with (but not limited to) these specific SEND, or your own young person has one of these SEND, then they may have difficulties with their fine motor skills.

▶ **Cerebral palsy** – The NHS (2023a) explains that there are four different types of cerebral palsy: spastic cerebral palsy, dyskinetic cerebral palsy, ataxic cerebral palsy and mixed cerebral palsy. Young people's motor skills may be affected differently depending on the type of cerebral palsy and the effect it has on the individual (which also varies). Young people with cerebral palsy may experience difficulties with coordination and balance, as well as muscle weakness, muscle stiffness and muscle spasms.

- **Developmental Coordination Disorder (DCD or dyspraxia)** – DCD effects fine motor skills but it's important to note that a young person with DCD may struggle with a whole range of aspects of motor planning and execution, including thinking of the idea, planning how to do it and then moving the body. Therefore, in addition to fine motor skill difficulties they may find organising themselves and their ideas difficult. (See Chapter 7 on *Concentration and Organisation Skills*.)

- **Dysgraphia** – Originating from the Greek words 'dys' meaning 'bad', and 'graphia' meaning 'handwriting', dysgraphia impacts on young people's handwriting – including letter size, spacing and formation. But its impacts aren't just limited to handwriting; young people with dysgraphia may find all aspects of fine motor skill activities difficult, from life skills such as using cutlery and tying shoe laces to academic skills such as measuring out liquids in food technology or science. Dysgraphia can also have impacts on a young person's concentration skills. (See Chapter 7 for further advice on this.)

- **Autism** – Some (but not all) autistic people may also have difficulties with their fine motor skills, particularly if they have a co-existing SEND that impacts motor skills.

- **Sensory processing differences** – As previously mentioned, there's a link between sensory input and motor skills development and, as a result, young people with sensory processing differences may also have difficulties with their motor skills. For further information on sensory processing differences, please read Chapter 5.

Other types of SEND linked to fine motor skill difficulties include:

- acquired brain injury
- developmental delay
- Down's syndrome
- muscular dystrophy
- hypermobility
- Ehlers-Danlos Syndrome (EDS)
- hydrocephalus
- FAS
- spina bifida.

WHAT YOU MIGHT NOTICE

If a young person isn't already on your radar for having one or more of the specific SEND listed above, how will you be able to identify that they have difficulties with fine motor skills? These are a few things to look out for. I've purposefully split these into things you may notice in the classroom versus those at home, as there are many that are very specific to the setting you are observing them in.

IN LESSONS

- **Behaviour** – Understandably, difficulties that impact on the student's ability to complete tasks independently, as well as get their ideas on paper, can be hugely frustrating. Therefore, it's no surprise that a young person with fine motor skill difficulties who isn't supported effectively may struggle with their behaviour in lessons. This could be by appearing uninterested and disengaged or more outwardly disruptive. It's also not just frustration at the particular task, but built-up frustration over time impacting on their self-esteem and view of learning.

- **Not writing 'enough'** – Students, due to their fine motor difficulties, might not be able to write as much as their peers in the same amount of time. This may, mistakenly, come across as them just not putting in enough effort to finish the task.

- **Fatigue during writing tasks** – Young people may have discomfort and fatigue when writing for longer periods of time. While a word processor is often advisable, please note that they may also get fatigued when typing as a result of fine motor difficulties.

- **Atypical pen grip** – Young people with fine motor difficulties may have an atypical pen grip. It's likely that by secondary school their pen grip is well established and would therefore be too difficult to change. However, it's worth noting that it could still cause them discomfort when writing for periods of time.

- **Handwriting** – Are they pressing too hard on the paper, or not hard enough? Are there differences in letter formation, size and spacing? Is their work difficult to read? And does their written work not match with their verbal ability? If so, it's likely that fine motor difficulties are impacting on their handwriting skills.

- **Difficulties in practical lessons/activities** – Many students enjoy practical elements of lessons and practical-based lessons in secondary school. But students with fine motor skill difficulties may find these sorts of activities challenging and frustrating. It could be that they find measuring in science, maths and food technology difficult. Or are nervous about cutting/chopping accurately in science and D&T respectively. You may also notice them lacking confidence and ability when using scissors or in any construction-based activity. And in maths, in particular, you may observe difficulties with manipulating equipment (ruler, compass, etc.). Be aware that as they get older, they may hide these difficulties by trying to avoid these types of activities so as not to draw attention to themselves.

AT HOME

- **Slower getting dressed** – Young people with fine motor skill difficulties are likely to take longer getting dressed and organising their school bag. They may/may not be able to tie their shoe laces. If they can, they might not tie them tightly enough meaning they are more likely to come loose throughout the day.

- **Difficulties texting** – Young people may find texting or posting on social media difficult due to the fine motor demands. This can cause frustration and fear of isolation from peers.

- **Frustration when gaming** – While some video games can have a positive impact on improving motor skills, and there are adaptable versions of many controllers to support people with motor skill difficulties (see *Resources*), you may find young people get frustrated easier while gaming due to the fine motor demands.

- **Using a knife and fork** – Young people with fine motor difficulties may struggle to use their cutlery correctly.

STRATEGIES

Here are some strategies for both school and home to support young people with fine motor skill difficulties and help them to further develop these skills. If a student receives support from an external professional, such as an occupational therapist (OT), ensure you are also implementing their suggestions of strategies. When supporting a young person with fine motor difficulties, our aim should be to set them up for success. To do this, we need to focus on what success in a task looks like, remove other barriers and provide them with opportunities to accomplish tasks themselves.

IN THE CLASSROOM

These strategies are designed specifically for the classroom, suitable for both teachers and teaching assistants.

▶ **Time** – Providing young people with fine motor skill difficulties with time allows them to have and gain independence. It's important to make sure the balance is there. We don't want to let young people struggle to complete tasks due to fine motor difficulties, but we also need to make sure we aren't too quick to support, robbing them of the opportunity to practise and their time to be independent. Often, discussing this sensitively with the young person can be helpful, asking when they need support and when they would like the autonomy to do something themselves, as practising some of these skills is really important.

▶ **Support at the start of tasks: don't finish off tasks for students** – A young person with fine motor skill difficulties may take longer than their peers to complete lesson tasks. As a result, they may traditionally be given support to finish off the task, perhaps after the lesson or with peer/TA support. Not getting the satisfaction of completing a task can be detrimental to a young person's self-esteem. One way around this is to try supporting at the *start* instead. For example, we could pre-start lesson activities for them (after discussion with the young person), to enable them to finish the last steps of an activity themselves, instead of supporting them to finish it and taking away that sense of achievement. In science, for example, this could be supporting them at the start to draw the axis of the graph to give them more time to accomplish plotting the results.

▶ **Adapt to reduce fine motor skills load** – There will be times when the work required in the lesson is reliant on student's fine motor skills, but it's important to question if there are ways you can adapt the lesson activities to reduce the pressure on fine motor skills. This might be changing a practical-based activity to make it less (unnecessarily) fiddly to enable all students to succeed. Or reducing the amount of extended writing in the lesson, if it's not linked to the objective, by allowing students to record their thoughts as bullet points instead to reduce muscle fatigue.

▶ **Increase size and scale** – Plotting on small graphs, labelling small diagrams, filling in tiny tables and completing worksheets with small boxes can be more challenging for children with fine motor skill difficulties and adds an extra barrier to their learning as they need to be precise with their writing placement. A simple way to support this is to enlarge the size of worksheets and tables and use graph paper with larger squares.

- **Use the technology** – There is some absolutely amazing technology out there that can support young people with fine motor skill difficulties and we shouldn't be afraid to try it. Not only does it help them now, but it provides them with experience of using this technology for later in life, helping them to be part of their toolkit of support when they are adults. Technology that can support includes (but is not limited to): speech-to-text software, word processors, tablets and video recording. For example, we can also utilise ICT to record practical work that doesn't need to be drawn/written (e.g. in a science experiment, in drama, dance or D&T). We can also use technology to simply reduce the amount a student needs to draw, for example, when drawing and labelling a diagram we could print it off just for them to label.

- **Pre-teach equipment skills** – We can support students with new equipment by giving more time and more opportunities to practise using them (perhaps even before the lesson). This would be important for subjects such as (but not limited to) art, science, D&T, PE. For example, in food technology, we could pre-teach the skill of grating.

ACROSS THE SCHOOL

While teachers can use strategies in the classroom to support children with fine motor skill difficulties, having a school-wide approach as well (led by the SENDCo and/or SLT) may enable more consistency. It's also worth noting that many strategies and whole-school approaches are likely to benefit all students and not just those with fine motor skill difficulties.

- **Ethos of understanding around adaptations** – Through staff training, school assemblies, communication of policies, student voice and peer support – develop an ethos across school (staff and students) of understanding and support for students who need certain adaptations, such as a word processor in lessons.

- **Involve students in decisions around accessibility** – Listen to students with fine motor skill difficulties and involve them in decisions (if they would like to be) around accessibility, strategies and equipment/resources.

- **Check and adapt equipment** – Check that equipment used across all subjects is accessible to students with fine motor skill difficulties and if it isn't, work out suitable adaptations (consult family, students and any external professionals if needed). Adaptations could include adding a pencil grip to some paint brushes in art, or changing the settings in ICT for particular students so that the cursor is larger.

▶ **Clubs to support fine motor practice** – Lunchtime or after-school clubs that enable students to practise skills in a safe environment can help to boost confidence as well as help to develop fine motor skills. Examples of clubs that would support fine motor skills include: cooking, baking, sewing, knitting, board games, chess club, LEGO®, music, pool (snooker) and perhaps (now more popular than ever, thanks to Luke Littler), darts.

▶ **Promote touch-typing** – To help students across school who may use word processors to record some of their written work due to fine motor skill difficulties, look at developing their touch-typing skills. This could be as an intervention or introducing free touch-typing activities during form time or as an activity suggestion to send home. One website that's particularly helpful is Typing Club.

AT HOME

There are many ways, as families, we can support young people with fine motor skill difficulties. The strategies below include examples of incorporating fine motor skill-building activities into daily routines, providing ample time and opportunities for practice and offering ways in which young people can use adaptive tools for increased accessibility. As always, if your young person is supported by external professionals for their fine motor skill difficulties, such as an occupational therapist (OT), be led by their expertise.

▶ **Give time** – Ensure young people have plenty of time for tasks such as getting dressed and organising their school bag. As difficult as it can be (and I really do appreciate this as I'm writing this!), when we/they are running late and we need them to hurry up, it's important to try to give them time to practise these skills without feeling under pressure as they are more likely to be able to succeed (boosting their self-esteem and helping them next time).

▶ **Opportunities** – Providing opportunities to further develop and practise fine motor skills can be helpful. The key is to integrate fine motor skill development into daily activities in a non-patronising way, similar to life skills. This ensures that young people see the benefit of these activities for developing independence and not as an extra 'fine motor skills' activity forced upon them. Life skill activities that also help fine motor skills include:

- **Helping with DIY** – With supervision, tasks such as using a screwdriver, selecting and passing over correct screws, bolts, etc. can be great for fine motor skills practice but also for developing other important skills. Ensure you risk assess based on your child's fine motor skills to make sure they are safe.
- **Laundry** – Sorting and pairing socks, hanging washing on the line using pegs and putting laundry away into drawers are all brilliant for fine motor skills practice as well as useful life skills.
- **Cooking** – Another really useful life skill that also provides opportunities for fine motor skills practice, with chopping, grating, stirring, pouring and measuring, for example. Again, we need to make sure we risk assess based on the young person's fine motor skills for more risky activities, such as cutting using a sharp knife, etc. Pizza or biscuit making whereby the young person needs to roll out and shape the dough, can be particularly useful for developing hand strength for some young people with fine motor skill difficulties.
- **Counting coins** – Asking your young person to sort and count loose change is another useful fine motor activity. You could make this more fun by going to an arcade with loose change.

▶ **Introduce hobbies and activities that support fine motor skills** – Here is a selection of activities/hobbies that can be helpful for fine motor skills practice. You know your child best, and activities in their free time are supposed to be fun – so if some of these will be too fiddly and frustrating, feel free to avoid! Instead, perhaps look at the list together and see if there are any they would like to try, to see if they enjoy them:

- Rubik's cube
- clay modelling
- making paper airplanes (there's lots of YouTube videos available to show you how to make really exciting types)
- jigsaws
- board games
- pegboard games (e.g. travel Monopoly, travel chess)
- Jenga
- pick-up sticks
- Hama beads

- jewellery making
- nail art
- painting
- drawing
- construction kits (e.g. Air-fix models)
- fishing
- loom bands
- card games.

▶ **Support with other options** – Practising fine motor skills is important, but not at the expense of self-esteem if fine motor skills are challenging. Look at preparing your child for adulthood as well as letting them enjoy being a teenager, by making tasks more accessible and allowing practice with adaptive tools. Examples include: adaptive shoe fastenings (velcro fastenings, elastic shoelaces, etc.), adaptive utensils, weighted pencils, etc. (see *Resources* for further ideas).

RESOURCES

▶ **Pen/pencil grips** – In my experience, while pen/pencil grips don't always resolve how a young person holds a pencil (especially as by this point their pencil/pen grip will likely be entrenched), they can be beneficial in some instances. It's crucial to use them in conjunction with other resources that support the root causes of their difficulties. When selecting a pen/pencil grip, the objective is to find one that enables the young person to write comfortably and effectively, rather than aiming for a perfect pencil grasp. There are a variety of pencil grips available, as well as pencils and pens that feature built-in grips. Young people may prefer to have one that has a grip inbuilt discreetly, to avoid being noticed by others.

▶ **Scissors** – For young people with fine motor skill difficulties, using regular scissors can be particularly challenging. There are various types of scissors designed to provide extra support:

- **Spring-loaded scissors** – Featuring a spring mechanism, these scissors automatically open after cutting, reducing the effort required and making cutting tasks easier.

- **Easy grip and long-loop scissors** – These lightweight scissors often reopen on their own, lessening fatigue. They may lack finger loops, allowing the young person to press with their thumb or palm, which is beneficial for those with reduced hand strength.

- **Dual-control scissors** – Designed for dual use, these scissors allow a teacher, assistant, parent or caregiver to assist a young person in cutting. The child uses the loops farthest from the blade, enabling guided cutting while improving fine motor skills, hand strength and coordination.

- **Tabletop scissors** – These innovative scissors rest on a table and can be operated by pressing down on a bar at the top to cut, with an automatic spring mechanism to reopen them. Some models can be mounted for added stability, making them ideal for young people who require one-handed scissors or have limited hand strength and fine motor control.

▶ **Pens, pencils and erasers:**

- **Pens with 'wetter' ink** – Pens like rollerballs and gel pens instead of a biro can be easier for young people to write with due to their runnier ink, which reduces the need to press hard and helps minimise fatigue, especially for those with hand strength difficulties.

- **Softer/harder pencils** – If a young person has limited hand strength or sensory processing differences, the pressure they apply while writing might be too little or too much. Using softer or harder pencils can help. Pencils vary in softness with 'B' being softer and 'H' being harder: 9B is very soft and dark, HB is medium and 9H is hard and light.

- **Triangular pencils** – These pencils have a triangular shape along their length, increasing contact with the fingers and promoting a comfortable writing position.

- **Jumbo/chunky pencils** – Larger, jumbo pencils can be easier to grip and more comfortable for some young people.

- **Easier/softer erasers** – Softer erasers are beneficial for young people with limited hand strength, allowing them to erase pencil marks successfully without pressing too hard.

- **Weighted pen/pencil toppers** – These add weight to the pen/pencil, providing more proprioceptive feedback, which helps young people apply the right pressure on the paper.

▶ **Writing slope** – A writing slope, which can be bought or improvised with a sturdy lever arch folder, helps support fine motor skills by encouraging a comfortable hand and wrist position for writing.

▶ **Dycem** – Dycem is a non-slip material designed to prevent equipment from sliding on surfaces, making it particularly useful in various educational and practical settings. For example, in science classrooms, it can be placed under lab equipment to ensure stability during experiments, reducing the risk of spills or accidents. This feature is especially beneficial for young people who may have difficulties with fine motor control, providing them with a more secure and manageable work environment. Dycem can also be used in other scenarios, such as under art supplies or cooking tools, to maintain a steady surface and enhance the ease of handling materials.

▶ **Adapted rulers** – These rulers are designed to make measuring and drawing easier for young people with fine motor skill difficulties. They may have built-in handles, non-slip bases and clear, easy-to-read measurements.

▶ **Larger lined/squared paper** – Larger squares on squared paper can make it easier for young people with fine motor skill difficulties to write/draw on (e.g. drawing a graph and annotating), as they don't need to reduce the size of their writing and have a larger scale to work on, making it less fiddly. The same is said for writing on paper with bigger spacing between the lines. There is also lined paper available that has raised lines providing tactile feedback to young people to help them stay within the lines when writing. These would also be useful for young people who are partially sighted.

▶ **Accessible computer adaptations** – Adapted keyboards and mouse can make computer use more accessible for young people with fine motor skill difficulties. They can include features such as larger keys, colour-coded layouts and ergonomic designs. Keyboards with larger keys can help those who struggle with precision and colour-coded keys can make it easier for young people to find the next key quicker. Trackballs, touchpads and joysticks can also make using the cursor easier. There are also settings in computers to change the size of the cursor on the screen.

▶ **Adaptive controllers for gaming** – Video games can play a large part in young people's lives and therefore it's also beneficial for us to look at how we make these accessible too. Both Xbox and Playstation 5 have adaptive controllers available to buy.

- **Handles, straps and grips** – Adaptive handles, straps and grips can significantly enhance the usability of everyday items for young people with fine motor skill difficulties. These modifications can be applied to various objects such as mugs, pens and toothbrushes to provide better control and comfort.

- **Name stamp for work** – A name stamp can be an incredibly useful tool for young people, especially those with fine motor skill difficulties, as it simplifies the task of labelling their work. Instead of having to write their name repeatedly on every single piece of work at school that is not in their book, which can be tiring and challenging, a name stamp allows for quick and consistent labelling of their paper-based work.

GROSS MOTOR SKILLS

As I explained at the beginning of this chapter, gross motor skills involve the use of larger, core-stabilising muscles, which are crucial for activities such as walking, running, climbing and jumping. These skills are also essential for sitting comfortably at a desk and writing, especially for longer periods of time.

WHY ARE THEY IMPORTANT?

Supporting students with difficulties in gross motor skills is essential for their overall physical and mental health and wellbeing. While their motor skills may limit or make some activities challenging, it is our role as parents/carers and teachers to adapt activities and provide the necessary support to ensure all young people can be as active as is possible for them.

Gross motor skills form the foundation for fine motor skills, and without strong core muscles and coordination, it becomes challenging for young people to practise the fine motor skills needed for tasks like writing and manipulating small objects. We therefore need to place as much value on gross motor skills practice as we do fine motor.

Additionally, as gross motor skills help enable young people to be more independent, difficulties with gross motor skills can impact a young person's friendships, mental health and wellbeing. Independence and social connections are crucial for teenagers, and it is important that we support them in achieving as much independence as possible and ensure they are fully included within their friendship groups and peer activities.

WHO MIGHT NEED FURTHER SUPPORT WITH GROSS MOTOR SKILLS?

In my experience, all young people will benefit from extra gross motor skills practice, but there are a whole range of SEND that may affect a young person's gross motor skills.

I stress 'may' as we must remember that everyone is unique and are certainly not defined by a SEND, and as such they will have their own individual strengths and challenges. But generally speaking, if you have students in your class with (but not limited to) the specific SEND below, or your own child has one of these SEND, then they may have difficulties with their gross motor skills:

- **DCD (dyspraxia)** – Young people with DCD may face challenges with motor planning and execution, which includes coming up with the idea, planning the action and then moving the body accordingly.

- **Autism** – Some autistic young people may also experience difficulties with their gross motor skills, although this is not universal.

- **Sensory processing differences** – Similar to fine motor skills, sensory processing differences can affect gross motor skills. Refer to Chapter 5 for more information and advice on this topic.

- **Cerebral palsy** – The NHS (2023a) explains that there are four different types of cerebral palsy: spastic cerebral palsy, dyskinetic cerebral palsy, ataxic cerebral palsy and mixed cerebral palsy. Young people's motor skills may be affected differently depending on the type of cerebral palsy and the affect it has on the individual (which also varies). Young people with cerebral palsy may experience difficulties with coordination and balance, as well as muscle weakness, muscle stiffness and muscle spasms.

Other types of SEND linked to gross motor skill difficulties are:

- acquired Brain Injury
- Down's syndrome
- muscular dystrophy
- hypermobility
- hypotonia
- spina bifida
- Global Developmental Delay (GDD)

- hydrocephalus
- Ehlers-Danlos Syndrome (EDS).

WHAT YOU MIGHT NOTICE

If a young person isn't on your radar for having potential gross motor difficulties because they haven't been diagnosed with one of the SEND listed above, then you might notice they have difficulties with some of the following:

- **Behaviour** – You will notice that I frequently mention behaviour as a potential indicator of underlying difficulties. There is always a reason behind a young person's behaviour, and it could be that they are frustrated by their gross motor skill difficulties and expressing this frustration through their actions. It's important to always consider the reasons behind behaviour.
- **Fatigue** – A young person with gross motor difficulties may become more fatigued during physical activities than their peers and might need to take more frequent breaks.
- **Difficulties with dynamic balance and coordination** – Dynamic balance is the ability to maintain balance while moving. Young people with difficulties in this area might frequently hurt themselves accidentally, bump into things or trip, especially on uneven surfaces or in changing environments. They may also be less likely to use their hands to break a fall, leading to more injuries.
- **Challenges with sporting activities** – Activities such as swimming, cycling and ball games can be particularly challenging for some young people with gross motor difficulties.
- **Unable to multitask** – They may struggle to perform more than one task at a time or to follow multi-step instructions.
- **Running style** – You might notice that their running style is less fluid compared to their peers.
- **Avoidance of new sporting activities** – Due to fear of failure, young people with gross motor skill difficulties might avoid trying new sports. This may come across as a lack of engagement in PE or extracurricular clubs. As Kat explained in the case study at the start of this chapter, be aware of the impact of motor skill difficulties in PE on young people's self-esteem.

- **Fidgeting and moving in their seat** – Sitting at a desk requires good postural control and gross motor skills. Young people may become fatigued and, as a result, fidget more frequently while working at a desk.

- **Posture** – Difficulty maintaining a good and comfortable posture might be noticeable, affecting their ability to sit for extended periods.

- **Breakages of equipment in practical lessons** – They might have more frequent accidents, breakages or difficulties when using equipment in practical lessons, such as in science labs.

- **Difficulty moving around science labs or computer rooms** – Navigating these environments can be challenging, as these rooms often have more obstacles and different layouts to other classrooms. You may notice they are slower to move around these rooms or more prone to accidents such as tripping.

STRATEGIES

Here are some strategies for supporting young people with gross motor skill difficulties both in school and at home. If a student receives support from an external professional, such as an occupational therapist (OT), make sure to implement their suggested strategies as well.

IN THE CLASSROOM

These strategies are designed specifically for the classroom, suitable for both teachers and teaching assistants.

- **Movement breaks** – Incorporate regular breaks in lessons that allow students to move and stretch to help reduce fatigue and increase focus. If this will disrupt your lesson, look at ways you can incorporate movement into the normal routine for some students with gross motor difficulties to allow them to stretch and move, for example, handing out worksheets/books.

- **Simplify instructions** – If you're asking a student to do a multi-step task that involves movement, break the instructions down and provide one instruction at a time. For example, instead of 'Please could you hand out the books and when you find your book can you bring it to the front of the classroom and put it on top of the green books on my desk', ask them to 'Please hand out the books', then once completed 'Find their book', etc.

- **Adapt activities** – Ensure all lesson activities are adapted to include students with gross motor skill difficulties. For example, adapting a science experiment to make sure a student (whose gross motor skill difficulties may make this activity difficult) is able to join in and thrive.
- **Accessibility** – Ensure equipment and the environment is accessible to all students. This includes thinking about the layout of desks, and if it will pose any difficulties for students to walk around, as well as setting rules to ensure bags, etc. are stored under tables to prevent trip hazards.
- **Posture in lessons** – Emphasise the importance of good sitting posture, especially for long periods:
  - feet flat on the floor
  - hips level with or slightly higher than knees
  - forearms resting flat on the table
  - eyes level with the top of the computer screen when using a computer.
- **Focus on progress, not competition** – During activities that include gross motor skills, encourage personal progress and effort, rather than competition.

ACROSS THE SCHOOL

While teachers can use strategies in the classroom to support children with gross motor skill difficulties, having a school-wide approach as well (led by the SENDCo and/or SLT) may enable more consistency. It's also worth noting that many strategies and whole-school approaches are likely to benefit all students and not just those with gross motor skill difficulties.

- **Ensure accessibility** – Audit and make changes needed to ensure the entire school environment is accessible to all students. This may include thinking about different furniture, ramps, accessible toilets and investing in adaptive equipment (especially for practical subjects such as PE, D&T, art, ICT and science, etc.).
- **Extracurricular activities** – Consider expanding lunchtime and after-school activities that cater to different interests and abilities, but also develop gross motor skills. Sporting activities that aren't as competitive, for example, may help make students who have

gross motor skill difficulties more likely to attend. These include climbing clubs, gym sessions with weights, yoga and martial arts.

▶ **Training** – Provide regular training for teachers and staff on how to support students with gross motor difficulties. Share good practice of teachers who are fantastic at supporting students with gross motor skill difficulties in their classroom. Look at the subject-specific barriers for students with gross motor skills and explore ways to support.

▶ **Family and student voice** – Ensure excellent communication with students and their families, allowing for open discussion on ways to further support and enhance their learning.

AT HOME

There are many ways as families we can support young people with gross motor skill difficulties. As always, if your young person is supported by external professionals for their gross motor difficulties, such as an occupational therapist (OT), be led by their expertise.

▶ **Simplify instructions** – If you're asking your child to do something that involves movement, for example, finding their phone upstairs and putting it on charge, give young people one instruction at a time to support them.

▶ **Engage in activities that offer resistance** – Activities that provide muscle resistance, such as trampoline jumping, swimming, weight training, climbing, gardening and bike riding, can be really useful for some children with gross motor skill difficulties. As Kat explained in the case study, for some young people with motor skill differences, understanding and empathy might make the biggest impact.

▶ **Less competitive sports** – Many teenagers with gross motor skill difficulties can become disengaged in competitive or team sports due to feeling self-conscious in front of their peers or being afraid of letting their team down. It may be worth exploring sports that are less competitive or not team sports for them to try, that also help with gross motor skills, for example, yoga, martial arts, skateboarding, go-karting, swimming and golf.

▶ **Games** – Use interactive games like dance mats to help develop gross motor skills through play. You could also introduce non-screen-based games such as Twister. All of these can be great for bilateral integration (the ability to coordinate both sides of the body in a controlled and efficient way).

- **Gym ball** – A novel, but useful activity you can introduce is sitting on a gym ball while watching TV to improve balance and core strength.
- **Pull-up bars** – Install pull-up bars at home for upper body strength exercises.

RESOURCES

As with fine motor skills, if a young person has input from an OT, make sure to consult them as to which resources would be best for that particular student. I would strongly recommend speaking to the student's family too (the experts!), as they may well have tried resources at home, so it is worth finding out which ones they have tried and which have worked. And definitely discuss with the young person before introducing any new resources; we need to consider how teenagers may feel using different resources in front of their peers.

AT SCHOOL AND/OR WORKING AT A DESK

- **Writing slope** – A writing slope can be purchased or made at home (some people use a strong lever arch folder). It is placed on the student's desk to rest their work on while writing. This helps support gross motor skills by promoting a comfortable writing posture.
- **Sitting wedge** – Placed on the student's chair, a sitting wedge helps them to maintain good posture while seated.
- **Wobble cushion** – Similar to the wedge, a wobble cushion encourages good posture and helps improve core stability through small movements. This can be particularly beneficial for students who need to move to concentrate.
- **Footrest** – If a young person's feet do not touch the floor while seated, a footrest can help them to maintain proper posture.
- **Standing desk** – Standing desks are excellent for students who require more movement to concentrate. They also benefit those who find it uncomfortable to sit for extended periods due to gross motor skill difficulties.

AT HOME AND/OR DURING SPORTS

- **Use larger and lighter balls/equipment** – For young people struggling with throwing and catching or other sports, using larger and lighter equipment can help. This might include a bigger, lighter ball or even a balloon, which falls more slowly and is easier to catch. You can also use larger or lower basketball nets and giant lightweight tennis rackets.

- **Balance board** – Balance boards (or wobble boards or rocker boards) are fun for young people to stand on and are great for balance, core strength and posture.

- **Trampoline** – Trampolines provide a safe environment for practising balancing and jumping, which are excellent for developing gross motor skills.

- **Space hopper** – Sitting and bouncing on a space hopper (or exercise ball) helps to develop core muscle strength and balance.

- **Bikes** – Riding a bike is not only great for social interaction (many young people enjoy cycling with friends) but also involves balance, multitasking, postural control and core strength.

FURTHER READING AND SUPPORT

Websites

Griffin OT website www.griffinot.com

Movement Matters www.movementmattersuk.org

SASC Guidance on DCD www.sasc.org.uk/media/m2snu21n/dcd-dyspraxia-sasc-guidance-march-2020.pdf

'The SEN Resources Blog' hosted by Georgina Durrant www.senresourcesblog.com

Touch-typing apps/software

Nessy Fingers Touch Typing www.nessy.com/en-gb/product/nessy-fingers-touch-typing-home

TypingClub www.typingclub.com

CHAPTER 5
SENSORY PROCESSING DIFFERENCES

CASE STUDY

SAPNA, 43, IS CURRENTLY WAITING FOR AN AUTISM DIAGNOSIS. HERE SHE REFLECTS ON SOME OF THE PROBLEMS SHE FACED IN SECONDARY SCHOOL WITH SENSORY PROCESSING DIFFERENCES AND SHARES HER INSIGHTS FROM THIS TIME.

Looking back, I think my struggles with my uniform impacted on my day at school. I was already masking but now my tactile sensitivity was impacting on how I felt internally.

Back in the early 90s, there was limited awareness of sensory processing and its impact on autistic people. In my secondary school, there was a strict uniform rule and our uniform had to be bought from specific shops with no flexibility.

The shirt had a specific collar which felt really heavy on my neckline. If the collar wasn't ironed properly, the feel of it would annoy me all day like an unscratched itch. The skirt was a classic style which was pleated but against the tights, it felt funny and I was always paranoid that it didn't swing properly and would ride up my legs. Along with an awful purse belt which always felt tight around my belly, I would have to wear tights which felt incredibly itchy and hot.

The school jumper wasn't any better and don't get me started on the heavy shoes! Imagine experiencing all these sensations before starting a full day at school. Imagine sitting on a desk trying to understand the *Lord of the Flies* while trying to fight the feelings of tightness and itchiness. Imagine trying to fit in amongst a group of competitive girls while resisting the urge to constantly rearrange your clothing.

Back in the day, I wish I was able to speak to someone about this rather than rebel against wearing the uniform and face the consequences. I would pick on the sleeves of my school jumper so it would fray and loosen. I would find any opportunity to wear trainers or soft top shoes including lying about having a foot condition. I would even write fake letters to not participate in PE lessons to avoid wearing tight PE kits or swimming hats. I was deceiving in order to cope and survive.

Even though there was a uniform policy, I wish adjustments could have been made for people with sensory processing difficulties. I wish there was the option to wear a sweatshirt or a polo shirt or maybe leggings rather than tights. I wish staff had the knowledge so they could have validated my feelings. Nowadays, schools provide lists of places where you can purchase clothes and shoes which have been endorsed by the National Autistic Society.

I now have an autistic son who attends a school where their uniform policy is relaxed for children with sensory needs so I am happy to see there is progress.

OVERVIEW OF NEED

Before we can look at differences in sensory processing and how we can support students, we first need to understand what sensory processing means and what it involves.

WHAT IS SENSORY PROCESSING?

Sensory processing refers to the complex way our brains interpret, organise and respond to the various signals received from sensory receptors throughout our bodies. These receptors are specialised cells capable of detecting external and internal stimuli. They are responsible for the way we experience the world around us and detect internal stimuli. Beyond the conventional five senses taught in school, our sensory system encompasses a range of additional senses. Here are the primary senses:

- **Sight** – Receptors in the back of the eyes detect light, enabling the brain to interpret patterns of light as movement and shapes.
- **Touch (tactile sense)** – Receptors in the skin detect various types of tactile stimuli, including pressure, pain, vibration and temperature. Certain areas of the skin have more of these receptors, which makes these areas of the skin more sensitive.
- **Hearing** – Sound is produced by air particle vibrations. When these vibrations reach the ear, they bounce off the outer ear and travel deeper into the inner ear, where receptors send auditory information to the brain.
- **Smell** – Olfactory receptors in the nose detect different chemical compounds, allowing us to perceive various odours.
- **Taste** – Gustatory receptors located in the mouth, particularly on the tongue, identify different taste sensations.
- **Interoception** – This collection of internal senses includes both conscious and unconscious perceptions, such as detecting the need to use the toilet or feeling hunger.
- **Vestibular sense** – The inner ear contains structures that provide our sense of balance. The vestibular system also supports other factors including postural control and spatial orientation.
- **Proprioception** – Specialised receptors in muscles and joints give us awareness of the position and movement of our body parts.

WHY ARE SENSORY PROCESSING DIFFERENCES IMPORTANT TO UNDERSTAND?

Different people process sensory information in different ways, and some students with certain types of SEND (diagnosed or not) may have certain sensory processing differences. Without support, sensory processing differences can make school and home life challenging. It is, therefore, absolutely vital that we ensure their sensory needs are met.

It can be difficult to imagine what it's like for someone else who processes sensory information differently to yourself, especially if it's not an area you've had training in. And of the many teachers who have had training in this area – according to a recent Teacher Tapp survey commissioned by TES – only ten per cent of secondary teachers felt that their teacher training/education meant they were well prepared to meet the needs of students with sensory needs (TES, 2024b).

However, if you are a teacher, understanding and supporting sensory differences is very important because, in my experience, you will likely have at least one student in each of your lessons who has differences and/or difficulties with sensory processing.

When learning about how different people process sensory information, one thing I think is really powerful is to stop and think about your own sensory experience and then think how it could differ if you processed this information in a different way.

For example, writing this I'm currently sitting at my desk, with the radio on in the background. Behind my laptop is a window with winter sunshine coming through. I'm a little cold but I'm wearing a warm, knitted jumper. I made a cup of coffee earlier, that is sat on a coaster next to me and I can smell the coffee ever so slightly.

I'm very aware that, while I'm comfortable and able to focus, someone else sitting in my chair may experience the sensory information differently to me. If they are hypersensitive (oversensitive) to stimuli, for example, they may find the radio too loud, the sunlight distracting, my woollen jumper itchy and maybe the coffee smell overpowering.

ACTIVITY

If you're a teacher, sit in your classroom and write down what you can see, hear, feel, smell.

(If you're a parent/carer, sit somewhere in the living space and do the same.)

_____
_____
_____

Now imagine you process sensory information in a different way, and write down how those things you see, hear and smell impact on your ability to focus.

_____
_____
_____

While these are examples of what it may be like for someone who is hypersensitive to stimuli, not all young people with sensory differences are more sensitive (hypersensitive/hyperresponsive). Some are *less* sensitive to sensory input (hyposensitive/hyporesponsive) and some are sensory *seeking* (where they seek out certain sensory input).

USEFUL DEFINITIONS

Hypersensitive – oversensitive to sensory stimuli.

Hyposensitive – decreased sensitivity to sensory stimuli.

Being hyposensitive to certain stimuli can bring its own difficulties for young people. It may be that their interoceptive sense is dampened and so they don't always recognise when they are hungry or thirsty. Or they are less sensitive to their proprioception sense and as a result appear more clumsy, knocking into others accidentally in the corridors, for example. When someone is hyposensitive to certain stimuli, they may also crave that sensory input; we call this 'sensory seeking'. Someone who is hyposensitive to vestibular input, for example, may crave/seek spinning, swinging movements. For younger children, this vestibular seeking may be more apparent with them cartwheeling across the living room at home, for example, but for teenagers this may come across in more subtle and age-appropriate ways making it harder to notice – such as a young person swinging their legs under the table or twisting round on the computer chairs.

Unfortunately, it is not quite as simple as someone being hypersensitive or hyposensitive to stimuli. Responses can vary depending on the stimuli and can fluctuate throughout the day and week. For example, a young person might be hypersensitive first thing in the morning when they are tired, but less so during the evening. Or, they might be hypersensitive to smells and struggle at lunchtime in the canteen as a result, but hyposensitive to sounds and feel the need to talk loudly or play music at a high volume. As such, each young person with sensory processing differences should be understood to be unique and we should tailor their support to their individual profile.

WHO MIGHT NEED FURTHER SUPPORT FOR THEIR SENSORY PROCESSING DIFFERENCES?

Although many people experience increased sensitivity to different stimuli at certain points in time, sensory processing difficulties are when it impacts on their day-to-day life and/or is present for the majority of the time. If this is the case, it's important to seek support from external professionals. In the United Kingdom, Sensory Processing Disorder (SPD) does not yet have an official diagnosis. However, an occupational therapist (OT) can identify sensory difficulties or differences. Young people with a diagnosed SEND may have sensory differences as part of the presentation of that particular SEND. For example, sensory differences are recognised as part of the diagnostic criteria for autism.

Young people with the following SEND may also have sensory differences (this list is not exhaustive):

- **Autism** – Many, although not all, autistic young people experience sensory processing differences. According to Chang et al. (2014), 'Over 90 per cent of children with Autism Spectrum Disorders (ASD) demonstrate atypical sensory behaviours'. It should be noted that sensory processing differences are not limited to an autistic person's childhood, but can impact on them throughout their lives.
- **Developmental Coordination Disorder (DCD or dyspraxia)** – DCD, a lifelong condition that makes movement and coordination difficult (including motor planning), affects around two to six per cent of school-aged children (Cleaton et al., 2020). In DCD, sensory differences can impact on planning and organisation of movements.
- **ADHD** – ADHD is referred to as a 'persistent pattern of inattention and/or hyperactivity-impulsivity that interferes with functioning or development' (NICE, 2025) and affects around five per cent of children worldwide (NICE, 2025). Some young people with ADHD have sensory differences. These sensory difficulties, in particular, sensory over-responsivity, have been linked to the anxiety that some young people with ADHD have (Ghanizadeh, 2011).
- **Down's syndrome** – Studies show that often children and young people with Down's syndrome have 'greater difficulties with

sensory processing than TD (typically developing) children' (Brugnaro et al., 2024).

Other types of SEND linked to sensory processing differences are:

- developmental delay
- speech delay
- cerebral palsy.

WHAT YOU MIGHT NOTICE

Young people without a specific diagnosed SEND might still encounter sensory differences. It may be that they have a specific SEND but are undiagnosed. As noted earlier, these differences in sensory processing can show up as hypersensitivity (being overly reactive), hyposensitivity (being underreactive) and sensory-seeking behaviours, or even a mix of these. It's important to remember that a student may be hypersensitive to some stimuli and hyposensitive to others, and this can change from one day to the next or even throughout a single day.

Below I have listed things you might observe in students who are hypersensitive, hyposensitive, or exhibit sensory-seeking behaviours (where they are less responsive to sensory input and seek more of it). But keep in mind, that each student's experience can be different and that it is a simplification to categorise sensory differences into hypersensitivity and hyposensitivity. (I've organised it like this in the book only to make it accessible.)

HYPERSENSITIVE

When a young person with sensory processing differences reaches secondary school age, it's likely that they will have developed some strategies to avoid certain sensory input that they find uncomfortable. This can sometimes make it harder to notice than in primary school-aged children. For example, a young person in primary school who is hypersensitive to lights, in particular, may have responded to being upset with bright lights, by covering their eyes if seated where the sun is shining on them, or even closing their eyes when it's bright. A teenager, however, who may be more self-conscious, may have found strategies to avoid this sensory input – such as choosing to wear sunglasses or a cap, or looking disengaged and putting their head in their hands if seated with the sun shining into the classroom upon them.

Here are some other things you may notice:

- **Touch** – They may not like having their hair cut, getting their hands dirty or touching ingredients when cooking. They may also dislike being touched by others – they might get upset if accidentally bumped into in the corridor, for example. They might find certain clothing (tights, blazers, shoes) or parts of clothing (labels, seams) itchy and uncomfortable. As Sapna explained at the start of the chapter, this may result in young people avoiding wearing school uniforms and PE kits.

- **Sounds** – They might find it difficult to concentrate with background noise from peers or equipment. They may tell others to be quiet during lessons, may withdraw from the lessons when it's loud or may hum to drown out the sound. They may be sensitive to sounds that some others aren't aware of, such as the buzz of lights or fan of the projector. They may also get very startled by loud sounds, such as the school bell or a teacher shouting unexpectedly. It is also worth looking up 'misophonia', which comes from the Greek words 'miso' meaning 'hate', and 'phonia' meaning 'sound'. While not currently an official diagnosis in the UK, it refers to people who are extremely sensitive to certain sounds, such as someone else eating. Students at school may be anxious going into the school canteen as a result of this, for example.

- **Lights** – As I mentioned earlier in the chapter, due to hypersensitivity to light, they may choose to wear sunglasses or a hat. Or they may look uncomfortable or withdrawn. Bright lights such as those from fluorescent lights can be particularly uncomfortable for some people with sensory processing differences.

- **Smells** – They may be more sensitive to smells, may be able to smell things that others can't, including perfumes, cooking smells from the canteen and food technology and chemicals in science.

- **Food (taste and/or texture)** – Many young people may stick to 'safe' foods and show reluctance to try new ones. They often prefer bland options and avoid anything with strong flavours or spices. The texture of foods can also be a challenge, as well as the unpredictability of certain foods' textures (such as blueberries, which can vary greatly depending on ripeness). This uncertainty can lead to the avoidance of such fruits. Consequently, some young people may end up with a limited diet. (It's important to note that this is not the only reason for a restricted diet.)

- **Vestibular input** – A young person who is hypersensitive to the vestibular sense may struggle with motion (travel) sickness (worth noting if they travel to school via a school bus, or for school trips), may have a fear of heights, they may appear 'clumsy' and off balance and dislike any movements in PE that involve balance/swinging/spinning.

- **Proprioceptive input** – A young person who is hypersensitive to the proprioceptive sense will be sensitive to whole-body movement and pressure. They may dislike physical contact, avoid physical activities in PE or during breaks, and find walking in busy places where they may get accidentally knocked overwhelming and upsetting.

- **Interoception input** – If a young person is hypersensitive to interoceptive input, they may be more acutely aware of hunger, thirst, needing the toilet and other internal discomforts such as stomach ache.

HYPOSENSITIVE

- **Proprioception** – Young people who are undersensitive to proprioception (where their body is in space) may accidentally bump into others or into furniture and door frames. As a teenager, this can get them into trouble with their peers who may not understand why they have knocked into them, or may result in unkind comments if they are appearing to be 'clumsy'. They may also 'not be aware of their own strength' and accidentally break equipment. Or they may have difficulty writing neatly due to putting too much/too little pressure on the paper with their pen.

- **Pain** – Some young people can be undersensitive to the feeling of pain and as a result have a high threshold for pain/discomfort. This could result in a young person not realising they have hurt themselves, or not comprehending and communicating the severity of an injury to get help. It can also result in others misunderstanding the severity of an injury based on their reaction.

- **Interoception** – Interoception is our internal senses, things like our feelings of hunger, needing the toilet and thirst. It also includes internal pain and again, some young people who are hyposensitive to interoception may have a high internal pain threshold. Being undersensitive to the interoceptive senses can also mean that young people aren't as aware when they need the toilet (and may get little warning), or don't eat/drink enough throughout the day because they haven't felt hungry or thirsty (hydration and nutrition can impact on health as well as ability to concentrate and learn).

- **Touch** – They might not be as aware of light touch.
- **Sounds** – They might be less likely to hear and respond to their name/instructions or other sounds in the environment.
- **Sight** – They might be less observant of things around them, may miss notices/signs/displays.
- **Smells** – They may not notice smells as easily as others.
- **Food (taste and/or texture)** – They might be able to eat very spicy or strong-flavoured foods.

SENSORY SEEKING

Sensory seeking means that a young person, due to their sensory processing differences, actively seeks out certain sensory inputs. You may notice:

- **Touch and proprioception** – They enjoy touching different materials, textures and surfaces. They may be quite physical with their peers (seeking touch and proprioceptive input) – giving hugs, fist bumps, high fives, patting on the shoulder, etc. with a lot of force. They might enjoy swinging/hanging from bars.
- **Sounds** – They may be generally loud, make loud noises, speak louder and enjoy things that make loud noises. They may also enjoy going to loud places like the cinema.
- **Vision** – They may love visual stimulation from sparkling, flashing lights or watching something moving quickly/spinning.
- **Food (taste and/or texture)** – They may enjoy trying new foods, especially ones with a lot of flavour, spice or crunchy textures.
- **Vestibular** – They may find it difficult to sit still, constantly moving around on their chair and rocking – seeking vestibular input. They may enjoy swinging, jumping and rollercoasters and fairground rides.

OTHER CONSIDERATIONS

Behaviour

Unmet sensory needs can present as a young person struggling with their behaviour in school and/or at home, for example. They may have got into trouble for being too rough, loud and physical with their peers when they are seeking sensory input. Or, if they are hyposensitive to sensory input, they might be getting told off in lessons for appearing to be disengaged and ignoring instructions.

One particular factor to be aware of is when a young person has reached sensory overload (or importantly, how to support them so they don't reach sensory overload). Sensory overload is the result of too much sensory input. This could be a result of walking down a busy, noisy corridor, for instance: hearing all the people talking, seeing the bright lights, being knocked into accidentally by others walking past, watching a large number of people walking past you, seeing all the displays and colours on the walls, etc. Another example is in supermarkets, shopping centres and train stations – with all the noises, displays, people, lights and smells.

Sensory overload can make people feel overwhelmed, find it difficult to make decisions and focus and can make them feel irritated, anxious and confused. It can also be exhausting having all that sensory input and make some people feel dizzy and even sick.

Sensory overload can also sometimes result in a meltdown (not to be confused with a tantrum) – in a meltdown people are not in control at all; or it can result in a shutdown (freeze response). Or they may experience both in different situations.

We must ensure we do our utmost as teachers and parents/carers to ensure a young person doesn't feel overloaded with sensory input and avoids a meltdown/shutdown. One way to help is to create an agreed plan on how to help a young person who is experiencing sensory overload, but it is key that we look at the triggers to *avoid* them being overwhelmed. There is a huge overlap between this chapter and Chapter 6 on emotional regulation, therefore, I would urge you to also read that chapter for ways to support children who are having a meltdown or shutdown.

Synaesthesia

This intriguing phenomenon involves a blending of the senses, where one sensory input (such as smell) can trigger another sense (like sound). For example, a young person with synaesthesia might experience a particular taste when seeing a specific colour.

STRATEGIES

The key approach for teachers and parents/carers is to recognise that sensory experiences differ from person to person. Just because *we* might find a room a pleasant temperature, not too noisy, or adequately lit, doesn't mean that everyone shares that experience! If you're a teacher with a class of students, some of whom have varying sensory needs, it can be challenging to create an optimal environment for everyone. Similarly, as a parent or carer of children with different sensory needs at home, achieving the right balance must be incredibly tough. However, there are steps you can take, adjustments you can make and resources you can use. The most important part is listening to the young person and putting in place changes that they would like to help them. And any interventions should be discussed with the young person and their family, and based on any advice from external professionals, ensuring they are tailored to those sensory requirements.

IN THE CLASSROOM

Strategies and changes will be unique for individual children with sensory processing differences; they may also be self-conscious of their needs and wish for strategies to be discreet; it's therefore important that any strategies are put in place in collaboration with them. Below are some suggestions to consider for each of the senses, split into if a young person is hypersensitive or hyposensitive/seeking for that particular sense:

SIGHT

Hypersensitive

- Seating away from bright ceiling lights and away from doors/windows.
- Using a desk divider to screen off any visual distractions that they don't wish to have when trying to focus.
- Changing classroom displays so that they are calmer and keeping them to a minimum (especially avoiding displays around the whiteboard so they can focus when looking at it).
- Avoid clutter in the classroom to reduce sensory overload.

Hyposensitive/seeking

- Light may be too dim, and they may prefer to sit in brightly lit areas such as by the window.
- Consider visuals and colours on worksheets.

SMELL AND TASTE

Hypersensitive

- Be mindful in lessons such as food technology and science (in particular) of some young peoples' hypersensitivity to smell. You can also help by opening windows to reduce smells. The same can

be said for the changing rooms in PE, especially with deodorants being sprayed.
- Avoid wearing perfume.
- Respect that they may not feel able to try new foods.

Hyposensitive/seeking

- If you have a young person who is sensory seeking new tastes and strong flavours, this could be a great opportunity to explore recipes during food technology, for example.

SOUND

Hypersensitive

- Give warnings before loud noises: this might be a discreet (pre-agreed) nod to them before speaking loudly to the whole class, or a heads up before planned fire alarms or the school bell (if you still use it – see page 101 for school bell alternatives).
- Try to reduce excessive chair noise (scraping across the floor); there are pads you can put under chairs to reduce this. It's also worth remembering young people with hypersensitivity to sound when you have need to move the desks in the lesson, allowing them to step out during this time if they would prefer.
- Be aware and look at ways to reduce noise for students with hypersensitivity to sound in lessons such as PE and D&T.

Hyposensitive/seeking

- Make sure you have gained their attention before speaking to them if they are undersensitive to sound, remembering *not* to tell them off if they appear 'not to be listening', as it may be their hyposensitivity instead.
- Provide sufficient wait time for processing auditory instructions.
- Support students with verbal instructions by providing accompanying visuals or written instructions.
- Check they have heard you by asking the young person to repeat the instruction back.

TOUCH

Hypersensitive

- Be mindful of tactile hypersensitivity in practical lessons, perhaps giving the option to wear gloves if a messy activity, or the option not to touch.

- Consider letting young people who are hypersensitive to touch stand at the front or end of the queue when lining up for anything, to reduce how much they are accidentally touched by others.

Hyposensitive/seeking

- Provide or allow students to touch sensory materials/fidget toys.
- Use social stories about personal space and hugging if they seek touch but it is causing problems with their peers.
- Risk assess during practical lessons in terms of their safety, if less aware of sensory input.

VESTIBULAR

Hypersensitive

- Be mindful of movements in PE that may be uncomfortable for students who are hypersensitive to vestibular movement.
- Be aware that students who are hypersensitive to vestibular input may experience travel sickness – this may be particularly important to consider if they are going on a school trip and if they travel to school by bus.

Hyposensitive/seeking

- Provide movement breaks, if practicable, that allow vestibular input.
- Explore using functional movement breaks, for example, handing out books, etc.
- In PE, consider vestibular movements that a young person who is seeking vestibular input might benefit from.

PROPRIOCEPTIVE

Hypersensitive

- Look at seating arrangements, allow a young person who is hypersensitive to proprioceptive input to not be seated in the main thoroughfare of the classroom or by the door (helping them to avoid bumps and knocks by others against their chair, etc).

Hyposensitive/seeking

- Provide functional 'heavy work activities' for young people who seek proprioceptive input – this might be asking if they could help carry and hand out books, for example.

- Consider the layout of the classroom, desks, etc. for young people who are hyposensitive to proprioceptive input, so they are less likely to accidentally knock into desks and chairs.

INTEROCEPTION

- **Awareness of physical needs** – If a student is hypersensitive or hyposensitive to interoception, it may affect their awareness of hunger, thirst and needing the toilet, which can impact on health and wellbeing. It's important to be aware of this and give reminders if necessary, particularly for drinks. Always allow access to water and toilets.

- **Temperature under/oversensitivity** – It is also vital that we are aware that sensory processing differences can affect how a young person experiences temperature and recognise that, while we may think it's not warm enough to need to open a window/pull down a blind/take off a blazer, that's just our perception; for them it may be. This needs to be respected.

ACROSS THE SCHOOL

It's not just the classroom environment and lesson that can be difficult for some young people with sensory processing differences, but the whole school environment. Everything from the noisy, narrow, busy corridors to the noise and smells of the school canteen. Therefore, in order to fully support young people with sensory processing differences in secondary school, we need to first look at approaches and changes across the whole school environment, led by SLT/SENDCo. It goes without saying that a school-wide approach (led by the SENDCo and/or SLT) should also enable more consistency.

It's also worth noting that many strategies and whole-school approaches are likely to benefit all students and not just those with known sensory processing differences.

- **Sensory audit** – First and foremost, spend some time completing a sensory audit of the entire school. There are lots of free sensory audits available online that you can print and complete, but essentially, you are checking for aspects of the school environment that may be problematic for young people with sensory processing differences, considering all the senses. For example, use of lights, busyness of the corridors, noises, smells, etc. Using this information, in partnership with students (student voice is key!), you can look at what changes can be made to make the school environment more accessible for students with sensory processing differences. Key changes that in my experience can make a significant difference include:

- **Scrap the school bell** – The school bell can be hugely problematic for many students with sensory processing differences: not only is it loud but it's also abrupt. It can also be stressful for students who find transitions difficult, as it can feel like it sounds 'without warning'. Because of this, many secondary schools have scrapped their school bell for lesson transitions and break/lunch and only use a bell for fire alarms and the end of the school day. Some schools haven't replaced their school bell with anything and, instead, use it as an opportunity to develop young people's life skills on time management – reflecting the 'real world'. Others have replaced with music, jingles and even student announcements.

- **Look at alternatives to hand dryers** – Hand dryers can cause similar problems for young people with sensory processing differences, especially if they are hypersensitive to sounds. Not only are they loud but they are often in small spaces, making them feel even more overstimulating. An easy swap is to consider paper towels or if not, a quieter hand dryer.

- **Ditch the fluorescent lights** – Fluorescent lights with their harsh lighting and background hum can create real problems for young people with sensory processing differences, from distraction to significant discomfort. Moving away from using these in schools and considering more appropriate lighting can make a big difference.

- **Flexibility on school uniform** – For young people who are hypersensitive to touch, school uniforms can present huge difficulties, impacting on their ability to focus in lessons, behaviour and even attendance, due to discomfort. Often items such as tights, school shoes, shirts/ties and blazers can be the most problematic (but it's important to be guided by the individual). And I'd advise providing flexibility for students with sensory differences on certain items of uniform. It's also worth noting that it's not just hypersensitivity to touch that can create difficulties with school uniform, but it's also about temperature regulation. Young people with sensory processing differences may experience the feeling of temperature differently and this should be respected. Flexibility to be able to take off their jumper when they are warm, or not wear tights when they feel too hot – not when it reaches a certain time of year/temperature – should be accepted and understood.

- **More soft furnishings** – Soft furnishings such as cushions, carpets and rugs (where safe to have) can absorb and dampen down excessive noises and can be a relatively cheap(ish) way of supporting students who are hypersensitive to noises.

- **Location of classrooms** – Moving across the school from one classroom to the next can be difficult for young people with sensory differences, with the busy corridors filled with lots of other students and noise. While I appreciate considering the location of classrooms for all subjects across the school is only going to be possible for a new build, there are things we can do for our newest of students to make the transition easier. A Year 7 base of classrooms can be created, where Year 7 remain for most of the school day (avoiding the hustle and bustle), with teachers (where appropriate and possible) moving to them to teach in their base. This isn't just an adjustment for students with sensory processing difficulties, but for all students who may find the transition of moving up to secondary school intimidating with worries around getting lost, busy corridors and being around older students.

- **Quiet space** – Creating a quiet space, potentially in the library, for students who need it during break and lunchtimes, can be a real positive change. Not everyone enjoys busy breaks and lunchtimes and some students need a break from the noise and crowds to regulate.

- **Sensory room** – Another space that can make a difference is a sensory room. These can be created with input from students and can be a great resource for students with sensory differences.

▶ **Individual sensory profile** – While whole-school changes are important and can make a big impact, it's also vital we consider the individual sensory needs of each student with sensory processing differences. A great way to do this can be to create individual sensory profiles (created in collaboration with the student and their family). A sensory profile helps to paint an accurate picture of a student's individual sensory differences and needs. It can show which sense they are hyper or hypo sensitive to and what support helps. While all support will be unique to the child, reasonable adjustments that may help include:

- **Corridor pass** – If a student is hypersensitive to noise/touch, having a pass – that allows a student to move between lessons at a different time when it's not busy and is therefore less noisy and they are less likely to be accidentally knocked/touched (e.g. five minutes before the end of the lesson) – can really help.

- **Lunch hall alternative** – For a student who is hypersensitive to smell, taste or noise, having a different (calmer) place to eat lunch can be helpful. If this isn't possible, consider giving an early pass for the canteen so they can avoid some of the noise.

- **Access to toilets and drinks** – As I explained earlier in the chapter, we have more than just our external senses but also our internal senses (interoception) and as such, students can be hyper or hypo sensitive to interoception. This can mean that they are more/less aware of when they need the toilet, for example, or need to drink. As both of these are fundamental to a young person's health and wellbeing, it's imperative that students have access to toilets when they need them and that toilets are not locked during lessons, and that they also have access to drinks.

▶ **After-school and lunchtime clubs** – Some young people with sensory processing differences, as I mentioned, seek sensory input, and one way to support these young people can be to create opportunities during and after school for these senses. A lovely way to do this is with clubs, for example, a music club for those seeking sound input or a climbing or trampolining club for those seeking vestibular/proprioceptive input.

▶ **Raise awareness** – It's unlikely that any of these measures will be successful without a whole-school approach to raising understanding, awareness and acceptance of sensory differences. Look at teaching students and training staff on sensory processing, to ensure an ethos of understanding of sensory differences is established. Part of this is also making sure all staff, in particular, staff involved in first aid, are aware of the differences in pain thresholds and tolerance. If a young person is hurt at school but due to their sensory differences doesn't react in the way you would expect (e.g. is quiet but not upset when they break a bone), it can pose a huge safeguarding issue if staff aren't aware of the variance in responses and experience for young people with sensory differences.

AT HOME

It goes without saying that sensory differences aren't going to be limited to school and, therefore, the role of the young person's family is paramount. If you're a parent or carer reading this, these strategies might help support your child, but *you* have the expertise on your own child and their needs, so pick and choose which ones will work best. You're also likely to already have a whole range of strategies that you have been using with them to support them since they were little, therefore these suggestions are here for you to consider as additional to what is already working. If you're a teacher/SENDCo, these could be strategies you share with the families of the students with sensory processing differences that you support.

The key to supporting a young person with sensory processing differences (or indeed any young person!) is to keep the lines of communication open, which I appreciate can be difficult for some during the teenage years. Keep talking to them about ways you can make things easier for them, at home and out and about, showing understanding. Sensory needs can fluctuate over time and may be more apparent during stressful situations such as exams and revision, therefore be open to flexibility and change with the support you already have in place. It might be an idea to complete a 'sensory audit' at home with your child, finding out what sensory triggers there are in the home that you can help reduce (some of these suggestions you'll find below split into each of the senses).

Another thing to consider is 'sensory play', and before you roll your eyes at me for suggesting you'll be able to tempt your teenager to partake in an activity usually designed for much younger children, let me explain. Sensory play often gets pigeonholed as a strategy for toddlers and younger children when actually we all partake in it just with a different name. When we think of ways we can relax, we might think of having a hot bath, or if it's sunny, relaxing on a chair in the sunshine in the garden, or listening to music, or maybe (if you're artistic) painting. We also partake in 'sensory play' not just to relax but when we want to feel more alert – this might be going to the gym, going for a run, having a cold shower. These are essentially adult versions of sensory play! Sensory because each of these involve/use some of the senses to either alert or relax us, with play meaning 'for enjoyment'. Help your young person to explore which 'sensory play' activity is most helpful for them. It's likely that they did lots of sensory play when they were younger and then stopped when the activities no longer felt age appropriate; bringing some of these back can make a huge difference and also provides them with lifelong strategies to help regulate their sensory inputs.

Here are some strategies and changes to consider for each of the senses, split into whether a young person is hypersensitive or hyposensitive/seeking for that particular sense:

SIGHT

Hypersensitive

- Help them to reduce clutter, especially in their bedroom, before sleeping.
- Help them to create a clear area for revision and homework.
- If possible and necessary, look together at changing the lighting in their room to help them focus/feel calm. Softer lighting from lamps, for example, can be more relaxing for some people.
- Reduce screen time before bed.

Hyposensitive/seeking

- Create a sensory-stimulating space together. This could include lights, a projector, music, etc.

SMELL AND TASTE

Hypersensitive

- Respect their need for 'safe foods' (being careful to ensure their dietary needs are met – if there are concerns around your child getting the correct nutrition and/or their weight, e.g. losing weight, it's important to speak to your GP and/dietician, or a speech and language therapist if there are concerns with swallowing and chewing).
- Consider the use of unscented soaps, shampoos, deodorants.
- Avoid diffusers, car air fresheners and strong-smelling cleaning products.
- Try tasteless kinds of toothpaste.

Hyposensitive/seeking

- Provide opportunities (if safe to do so) for them to cook at home – experiment together with new flavours and spices.
- Try candle- or soap-making together.
- Schedule time for them to have a long bath with scented soap.
- Encourage gardening and flower-arranging.

SOUND

Hypersensitive

- Carpets, rugs and cushions can be really helpful at dampening down sounds.

- Try to create (if practically possible) a quiet space in your house that they can retreat to.
- See if listening to white noise is helpful for them to relax or focus.
- Prepare for busy, noisy places – plan together what to do when they are out and about if the environment becomes too overstimulating for them. Think about what they can bring to help. Explore if they qualify for a sunflower lanyard for busy places like airports and theme parks. Look for quiet, sensory-friendly times/hours that cinemas and supermarkets (and other public places) have.

Hyposensitive/seeking

- Encourage listening to music.
- Provide opportunities for them to make music, perhaps trying a musical instrument if they want to.
- See if they would like to try listening to a podcast or music before bed to help them to sleep.

TOUCH

Hypersensitive

- A lot of the guidance around hypersensitivity to touch is on understanding that a young person may experience touch in a different way to you and what may feel like gentle pressure, for example, could be painful or cause discomfort to them, and believing and advocating for their experience is important. The general consensus is that we should not force young people who are hypersensitive to touch to complete an activity that involves the tactile sense, but not to avoid all tactical experiences and instead continue to offer opportunities. Things to consider:
    - **Labels on clothes** – Cutting these out can make a huge difference. If your child is able to, teach them how to do this with you for when they are adults.
    - **Texture of clothes** – Some textures like wool/fleece can feel uncomfortable for young people with sensory differences.
- **Hair cuts** – This can be an area that causes a lot of difficulties and anxiety for young people with sensory processing differences. Things to try could include: 'autism-friendly' hairdressers (ones that advertise themselves as putting in place changes to make it

a less sensory-overwhelming experience), mobile hairdressers, taking a mobile device/headphones for distraction, using a weighted lap pad and choosing a hairstyle that requires less maintenance.

- **Brushing hair** – Encourage brushing in front of a mirror – this can make the feeling of brushing hair more predictable and therefore slightly easier to manage.
- **Ask before hugs** – Create an understanding within your family and close friends to ask permission for hugs.

Hyposensitive/seeking

- Use weighted blankets and tactile resources (see *Resources* section for ideas).
- Encourage art and craft activities – tactile activities such as clay modelling, knitting, etc. all involve sensory input.
- Baking, especially that which involves kneading and rolling dough (for example, when making biscuits and bread).
- Encourage them to help with car washing, window cleaning and watering the garden (essentially age-appropriate and practical water play!).
- Consider clothing that is tight such as leggings to give more sensory input that they are seeking.

VESTIBULAR

Hypersensitive

- Support for travel sickness – encourage them to sit facing forwards in vehicles, not looking at mobile devices or reading. Sometimes fresh air through a slightly open window can also help.
- Avoid certain computer games that can cause motion sickness.
- Understand that hypersensitivity to vestibular input may cause/add to a genuine fear of heights.

Hyposensitive/seeking

- Provide opportunities to explore yoga and dance.
- Encourage activities that provide vestibular input, such as jumping on a trampoline, using a balance board and gymnastics.
- Try bilateral activities such as climbing and cycling.
- Use an exercise ball/space hopper.

PROPRIOCEPTION

Hypersensitive

▶ Respect their wishes not to hug or be hugged.

▶ Help them to avoid busy situations; these could be where they might be accidentally knocked into, e.g. crowded places and queues. Again it may be worth looking into the sunflower lanyard scheme and seeing if they qualify. Research designated 'sensory-friendly' or 'autism-friendly'/quiet times for going to the supermarket and other busy places.

Hyposensitive/seeking

▶ Provide opportunities for proprioceptive input such as yoga, stretching and hill walking, as well as 'heavy work' activities such as carrying shopping, pushing the wheelbarrow in the garden, etc.

▶ Support them in understanding that others may not like rough play and physical contact.

INTEROCEPTION

▶ **Hunger/thirst** – If a young person is hypersensitive or hyposensitive to interoception, it may affect their awareness of hunger and thirst. Establishing a routine or reminders for meals and drinks can be beneficial. Additionally, discussing feelings related to hunger, thirst, temperature (too hot, too cold), etc., can help them to understand and manage their sensations. For example, if you miss lunch, explain how it makes you feel, describing sensations in your stomach and how it may also affect your mood.

▶ **Temperature over/undersensitivity** – If they are less aware of temperature changes, clearly and verbally explain why you're moving into the shade on a hot day, wearing a cap, or removing a jumper. It's important to accept that they may experience different levels of discomfort at varying temperatures. For instance, if they say they're too warm while helping with DIY outside, even if you don't feel warm, acknowledge that they may perceive temperatures differently.

RESOURCES

- **Acoustic panelling** – These are sound-absorbing panels that can be placed on walls, ceilings and other surfaces to decrease noise levels. You can get some brilliant ones that just look like canvases. Some schools place these in classrooms, corridors, lunch halls and meeting rooms to dampen and absorb sounds. They are particularly beneficial for young people with sensory processing differences who find noise overwhelming

- **Weighted pen toppers** – These make the pen heavier, therefore providing more proprioceptive input to the young person when writing. This can support them in putting the right pressure on the paper, making their handwriting more legible.

- **Wobble cushion** – These air-filled cushions can be placed on a young person's seat, allowing for gentle movement while sitting. This subtle motion can help with focus, attention and sensory integration. When students use wobble cushions on their seats, they activate their core muscles to maintain balance, which enhances posture and overall sensory regulation. In my experience, wobble cushions are particularly beneficial for students needing additional sensory input to stay focused during lessons. The biggest downside to wobble cushions in secondary school, however, is that students can, understandably, sometimes feel self-conscious about using one and prefer just to use it for smaller intervention classes or at home for homework.

- **Standing desk** – When you are standing, often without realising, you make regular small movements to keep yourself in the standing position. These can be great for young people who need this input to concentrate.

- **Weighted blanket** – These specialised blankets are designed to be placed on the body, providing gentle pressure on the joints and muscles. This pressure can be especially helpful for students who need proprioceptive input to feel more grounded and focused. It's important to follow safety guidelines when using these blankets, as they are not intended for sleeping. Again be guided by the young person; they may prefer to use this type of resource at home. Other weighted resources to consider are weighted vests and weighted lap pads.

- **Sensory space resources** – These resources are for young people who benefit from sensory resources either to stimulate or to calm. They can be used at school in a sensory/calm area and/or at home. Often the best sensory spaces are created in collaboration with the young people who use them, helping to provide guidance on which resources they prefer and, if the purpose of the space is to be calming/stimulating, which senses the space should target. Visual sensory resources could include bubble tubes, fairy lights and light projectors, for example.

- **Ear defenders** – Young people who are hypersensitive to sound can wear these to dampen it down. Similarly, they may choose noise-cancelling headphones playing white noise or low-level music, or simple ear plugs to reduce the sound.
- **Chewable jewellery** – There is a wide variety of chewable jewellery available, offering discreet and accessible sensory input options. Another option is a 'chewable pen topper' – which, as the name suggests, sits on top of a pen for a young person to chew to access that sensory input they may be seeking. Alternatively, for out of school, you could look at hard sweets, chewing gum (if safe) or straws in drinks to chew.
- **Chair band** – These stretchy bands can be placed on the front legs of a chair, enabling students to push and pull their feet against the band during lessons or at home at the dinner table/doing homework. It provides sensory input enabling some young people to focus.
- **Body sock** – Body socks/sensory socks are made from stretchy materials and can be worn over the body. They offer deep pressure, proprioceptive and tactile sensory input which can be relaxing for some young people who are hyposensitive/sensory seeking these senses.
- **Desk screen** – For a young person who is hypersensitive to visual stimuli, having a desk screen/divider can be helpful for them to screen out distractions and focus on their work.
- **Reminder watch** – For young people who struggle with interoception and may find it difficult to know when to go to the toilet, have a drink, or remember to eat, you can purchase watches with vibrating reminders. An alternative would be using their smartphone (if they have one) to give them reminders. There are also water bottles with reminders of times written on the side, as a non-tech version to help remember to drink.

FURTHER READING AND SUPPORT

Websites

'Autism and sensory processing' by National Autistic Society 👆 www.autism.org.uk/advice-and-guidance/topics/about-autism/sensory-processing

'Sensory processing in young people with a learning disability and/or ASD' by CAHMS 👆 www.camhsnorthderbyshire.nhs.uk/learning-disabilities-sensory-processing

'Sensory processing: a guide for parents' by CEREBRA 👆 https://cerebra.org.uk/wp-content/uploads/2024/08/Sensory-processing-2024.pdf

'Ready to learn: interoception kit' by Government of South Australia 👆 www.positivepartnerships.com.au/uploads/PDF-files/Ready-to-learn-interoception-kit.pdf

Beacon House Therapeutic Services and Trauma Team website 👆 www.beaconhouse.org.uk

The Sensory Projects 👆 www.thesensoryprojects.co.uk

National Autistic Society 👆 www.autism.org.uk

Books

The Body Keeps The Score: Brain, Mind, and Body in the Healing of Trauma by Bessel van der Kolk

CHAPTER 6
EMOTIONAL REGULATION

CASE STUDY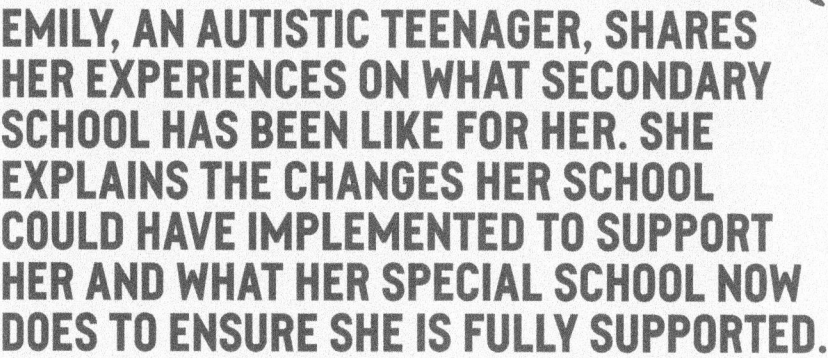

EMILY, AN AUTISTIC TEENAGER, SHARES HER EXPERIENCES ON WHAT SECONDARY SCHOOL HAS BEEN LIKE FOR HER. SHE EXPLAINS THE CHANGES HER SCHOOL COULD HAVE IMPLEMENTED TO SUPPORT HER AND WHAT HER SPECIAL SCHOOL NOW DOES TO ENSURE SHE IS FULLY SUPPORTED.

My name is Emily and I was diagnosed with autism in January 2024. I always struggled with friendships during primary school, especially in Key Stage 2, and then it became even more difficult when I was at high school. My autism means that I find it hard to read people, to understand what they mean, as often people don't say what they mean or do what they say. I have sensory differences that mean I struggle with busy, noisy places and I get easily overwhelmed. I don't like certain textures in clothes or food, I struggle to sleep and I am really sensitive to the way people talk to me. My mum and I have researched RSD (rejection-sensitive dysphoria) and I am sure this is me.

I managed to succeed at primary and high school in Years 7 and 8 by working really hard and being a perfectionist. I would come home and rewrite out my learning using highlighters and colours, trying to make it perfect. I always felt anxious but didn't realise what it was until school became impossible to attend.

I attend CAMHS twice a week for DBT with a clinical psychologist, to try to help me understand the trauma I have experienced, and once a fortnight to see my mental health practitioner.

To support me better, the school could have:

- spent time talking to me and listening to me
- created trusting relationships with me
- made sure things were predictable when room changes or teacher changes happened – to prepare me and alert me
- arranged for someone to meet me every morning to help me come into school and to go through my timetable in a positive, connected way, where they got to know me and what I really thought and felt
- had someone for me to go and talk to when I felt anxious, who wasn't too busy or didn't make me feel like a pain or a bother
- made sure something happened if it was promised, for example, if you said someone could go home if they needed to, then making sure that happened and that it wasn't dependent on a particular person being there to agree on it
- made sure I knew that you believed me and didn't compare my feelings or situation to someone who you thought had it worse
- connected with me to make sure I felt safe and liked – if people don't smile at me, I perceive they don't like me or they are angry
- found different ways for me to learn
- understood the impact of me feeling judged by others
- supported me to communicate my thoughts and feelings in a way that I could tell you how much I was struggling.

Things my special school does now that help me:

- They allow time to talk and time to listen.
- They provide someone to walk with me to class and to go into class with sometimes.
- The classes are smaller.
- There are quiet break-out rooms and igloos in the corridor.
- They listen to your needs and do as much as they can to help you.
- They let me into the hall to pace when I need to.
- They let me do work experience at a primary school in reception every Wednesday which I love.
- They let me cook even when it isn't a cooking lesson if I am overwhelmed/overstimulated.
- They let me draw and paint in the Art room when I need to feel calm.
- Teachers tell you their neuro differences – I have a teacher who is autistic and we talk about this.
- No one holds grudges – every day is a fresh start.
- You don't have to go outside at playtime; you can stay in and you can eat lunch in a small room.
- The teachers eat with you.
- If you have trouble eating in front of people, there is a small room you can eat in and they will get your food for you if you struggle.
- They have animals like goats and rabbits and chickens.
- You don't have to wear a strict uniform – we wear any leggings/tracksuits and a polo shirt with the school name on.
- There is a gym you can use.
- You don't have to get changed for PE.
- You can wear make-up and have nail varnish on if you need to (which I do in order to feel able to be at school).
- They text me if I can't be in school to check up and connect with me.
- The staff build really strong relationships with me and they don't blame me if I struggle or have a meltdown.
- They worked with me to create my own timetable and didn't make me do all the subjects when I was too overwhelmed.

CASE STUDY

JOE FAULTLEY, AN AUTISTIC AND NEURODIVERGENT ADVOCATE, REFLECTS ON HIS EXPERIENCE OF SECONDARY SCHOOL.

I'm passionate about supporting teachers and other professionals in education to develop how they communicate with and support autistic children and young people. For a significant part of my childhood, I was non-verbal and could not communicate verbally about my emotions, how being in school made me feel and what support I needed. Anxiety was, and remains, a powerful emotion and should never be underestimated.

Autistic people are more likely to experience higher levels of anxiety daily as they must navigate a complicated and often confusing sensory and social world. During secondary school, anxiety was constant throughout and too often became so overwhelming and unmanageable that it forced me to be regularly absent and unwell. Anxiety for me personally was triggered by the intense sensory environment of the school, together with specific lessons that involved physical coordination that never worked for me due to my dyspraxia (I absolutely hated any PE or sports lessons) and other situations that made a detrimental impact on my emotional regulation (e.g. being in large, noisy crowds of students).

With the general sensory environment being stressful enough, my anxiety and emotional regulation was made far worse by, sadly, a large majority of staff at secondary school not being flexible enough in their approaches and not understanding the seriousness of my anxiety, including how this impacted my overall mental health and wellbeing and ability to learn and process information at school. Although there were some excellent staff who did support me, sadly it's the negative experiences that stand out the most and made the most impact.

Not all autistic people may be able to speak or articulate how they are feeling when their anxiety becomes too high. It is important to make the most of visual tools such as alert cards to describe different emotions. It is important for autistic students to have access to a dedicated quiet space where they can de-stress. Having a 'time-out card', to alert staff that they need to have some time out of the room when their anxiety increases, is a useful idea.

Managing extreme fatigue and burnout caused by anxiety and sensory overwhelm was also a constant process during my time at secondary school. To support autistic students, it helps to allow time for rest breaks and activities, or interests that re-energise and promote relaxation.

It is very important for teachers to avoid making assumptions: an autistic student who is intelligent may still have significant needs affecting their daily life. No one person is the same – take time to listen and find out what reasonable adjustments they might need. Understanding what works best for your students as individuals is essential. For example, an adjustment could be to enable the student to leave the room slightly earlier so they can avoid the crowds. Small changes to your environment can make a big difference.

OVERVIEW OF NEED

WHAT IS EMOTIONAL REGULATION?

Emotional regulation is all about being able to manage emotions in a healthy way. It's about being able to develop a toolkit of strategies to draw on to help understand and navigate difficult feelings, changes and situations. And to express these emotions in a healthy way.

Emotional regulation is also developmental. And we must be mindful that a young person's developmental age and stage may not be the same as their chronological age and, as such, they may need more support with emotional regulation.

Developmentally, emotional regulation begins with the co-regulation of emotion. This is where a child relies on a trusted adult to help them regulate their emotions. This may be as a baby when a parent/carer rocks them back to sleep when they cry. Or it could be as a toddler when they fall over, graze their knee and get a hug. Or maybe as a child when they come home from school upset and a parent/carer sits with them, puts their arm around them and helps them to go through their feelings, offering advice.

As children develop, they start to self-regulate their emotions, which is where they begin to manage their emotions themselves.

As teachers, parents and carers, we support children and young people by co-regulating their emotions, with the aim to get them to the stage where they can also self-regulate their emotions.

According to research, it is expected that typically developing children will be able to regulate their emotions between the ages of 10 and 12 (Alarcón-Espinoza et al., 2023). This doesn't mean that they will never need support and co-regulation though, as there are plenty of adults that struggle to self-regulate their emotions. It is, therefore, important for all young people to have ongoing support.

WHO MIGHT NEED FURTHER SUPPORT WITH THEIR EMOTIONAL REGULATION?

For some children, emotional regulation will be inherently more difficult. This may be due to their developmental age, meaning they are not yet ready to be able to regulate their emotions themselves. It may be due to a specific SEND that impacts on emotions (see below). Or it may be that their basic needs have not been met (which I will discuss later), impacting on their ability to regulate their feelings.

It may be because, even with the best will in the world, a toolkit of emotional regulation strategies isn't enough to factor against the difficult lives some young people have already experienced.

Experiencing trauma or Adverse Childhood Experiences (ACEs) can influence a young person's ability to manage their emotions effectively (Tanner & Francis, 2025). They might develop unhealthy ways of reacting to situations as an adaptation to perceived threats. Even ACEs that occur before a young person can remember them can affect their emotional development. It's crucial for young people to feel secure. When they don't, they may remain in a constant state of fight or flight, which impacts various aspects of their life, including emotional regulation.

In terms of SEND, there are a whole range of SEND that may affect a young person's ability to regulate their emotions. I stress 'may', as we must remember that all young people are unique and are certainly not defined by their SEND, and as such they will have their own individual strengths and challenges. But generally speaking, if you have students in your class with (but not limited to) the specific SEND listed below, or your own child has one of these SEND, then they may have difficulties with their emotional regulation skills:

- ▶ **Autism** – Some autistic young people may struggle with emotional regulation. They can experience meltdowns or shutdowns due to emotional dysregulation or sensory overload. There are common myths about autism and emotions, such as the false belief that autistic individuals do not experience emotions or lack empathy. In fact, many autistic young people show significant empathy, sometimes more than their neurotypical peers. However, some autistic individuals may find it challenging to identify their emotions (see *Alexithymia* later on in this chapter). Note that strategies helpful for autistic individuals may not work for those with Pathological Demand Avoidance (PDA). For more information, research the PANDA approach as explained by the PDA Society.

▶ **ADHD** – Many young people with ADHD experience emotional dysregulation; studies have shown that this is the case for 25–45 per cent of young people with ADHD (Shaw *et al.*, 2014). Young people with ADHD may be hyperresponsive to emotions (feeling both positive and negative emotions more strongly), their mood may change quickly, and they may experience outbursts of strong emotional responses (Hirsch *et al.*, 2019).

▶ **Speech, language and communication needs (SLCN)** – Understandably, young people who find it difficult to express their feelings, wants and needs due to SLCN may feel frustrated and, as a result, find it difficult to regulate their emotions. As I explained in Chapter 1, many young people who we may have identified as having SEMH needs may, in fact, have unmet SLCN. Studies show that eight in ten children with 'emotional and behaviour disorders' have unidentified language difficulties (Hollo et al., 2014).

▶ **Developmental delay** – Developmental delays can mean that young people are emotionally younger than their peers. This can make it harder for them to co-regulate and self-regulate their emotions.

OTHER CONSIDERATIONS

Special educational needs not met

While I've listed some SEND that can inherently make emotional regulation more challenging, you could argue that *any* SEND (even if not directly linked to difficulties with emotional regulation) has the potential to impact a young person's ability to regulate their emotions if there isn't the correct support put in place. For example, dyslexia doesn't cause emotional regulation difficulties as such. However, a dyslexic teenager who is undiagnosed and misunderstood may experience emotional dysregulation due to a lack of support in school.

Tiredness

Quality sleep is essential for effectively regulating emotions. Being tired can make it much more difficult to respond to situations and feelings healthily. Certain types of SEND, such as ADHD, can significantly impact a young person's ability to fall asleep and stay asleep. Factors like disturbances from siblings and colder household temperatures can also affect sleep quality. Teenagers, in particular, face additional challenges – screen time from mobile phones, social media notifications and gaming in the bedroom can all disrupt sleep patterns. Furthermore, consuming caffeine or sugary foods and drinks before bed can negatively impact sleep. Hormonal changes and stress can also impact on tiredness (NHS, 2023c).

Hunger

Hunger can make it harder to manage emotions. Even missing a meal can lead to irritability and feeling short-tempered.

Low self-esteem

Low self-esteem, influenced by various factors including SEND, can affect a young person's ability to regulate their emotions.

WHAT YOU MIGHT NOTICE

OR WHAT YOU MIGHT NOT NOTICE

When you think of a young person struggling with emotional regulation, what do you think of? Quite often, the picture that comes to mind is a young person who is angry and lashing out. And while this certainly is how some young people with difficulties regulating their emotions might present, we must not forget the other young people who may be quieter, more withdrawn, or even appear to be absolutely 'fine' in school.

There will be some students in your school who are struggling with emotional regulation and are completely under the radar. They may be the ones who are bottling up their feelings and repressing them all day, perhaps behind a smile until they get home, where they let out their true feelings. This is called 'masking' and it is where a person subconsciously or consciously hides their feelings in different situations. For example, some autistic individuals might mask. Understandably, this can be exhausting and can impact their mental health and overall wellbeing.

Imagine you're at school, and there are many things throughout the day that bother you. But instead of reacting right away, you hold it in. Then, when you get home – our safe space with trusted people – you finally release those emotions, perhaps with a meltdown. To someone else, this meltdown might look like it was triggered by something minor when, in fact, it was the cumulative effect of the entire day. This phenomenon is known as the 'Coke bottle effect': think of yourself carrying a Coke bottle all day. Each time something upsets you, the bottle gets shaken. When you finally get home and open it, the Coke bursts out everywhere, much like pent-up emotions being released. At school, it might seem like everything's fine because you're masking your feelings. But often, the advice given is to change something at home since you appear okay in school. The reality is that school might be the source of stress, and you only feel safe expressing your true self at home. Therefore, as teachers, it's crucial to listen to parents and carers without judgement, and work together to identify possible triggers at school causing emotional difficulties at home.

WHAT TO LOOK OUT FOR

All young people are unique and, therefore, young people who need extra support regulating their emotions will present in a range of different ways, including (but not limited to) some of the following:

- **Struggling to stay calm** – Some young people might find it harder to stay calm and have bigger responses than their peers to seemingly minor problems. They may be more sensitive to changes and appear to be on high alert for long periods of time. They may respond to situations with aggression.

- **Withdrawn behaviour** – Conversely, some young people who are struggling with emotional regulation might be withdrawn. They may come across as low, tired, sad or uninterested.

- **Anxiety and worry** – Young people may experience more worries than others and need more reassurance. They may experience anxiety.

- **Difficulty focusing** – Due to being constantly on high alert, they may find it hard to concentrate, seem distracted and often forget things. This may at first be mistaken for a young person who's not engaged in the lesson at school.

- **Friendship challenges** – Emotional responses can make it tough for young people to make and maintain friendships and relationships. They may be more likely to fall out with their friends and may become socially isolated.

- **Avoiding conflict with peers** – Young people with emotional regulation difficulties may find it difficult to resolve conflicts and disagreements and, as a result, they may flee from situations where conflict arises. This can be much more difficult to notice than a young person who is falling out with their peers.

- **Walking out of lessons** – Similarly, if a young person struggles to resolve conflicts and flees from these situations, they may also be likely to walk out of lessons when upset.

- **Meltdowns** – When emotions become too much to deal with and a young person is overwhelmed by a situation, they might have a meltdown. Autistic individuals may experience meltdowns, however, they are not limited to just autistic people. Meltdowns can be triggered by a range of things that will be unique to the individual. It could include sensory overload, anxiety, or changes in routine. Meltdowns are not the same as a tantrum, as the young person is by no means in control of this response. The best way, I believe, is to think about them as a panic attack. In the same way as a panic attack, a young person during a meltdown is unlikely to be able to communicate, understand the situation, hear you properly or make sense of what you are telling them. Instead, your role as an adult is to focus on ensuring the young person is safe during the meltdown and to provide support afterwards to recover, removing any obvious triggers.

- **Shutdowns** – Like meltdowns, shutdowns happen when someone is overwhelmed, but instead of lashing out, they may withdraw, stay still and stop communicating. Autistic young people might experience shutdowns. Shutdowns can also be experienced after a meltdown, and it may seem like they've recovered, but they're still processing the overwhelm.

OTHER CONSIDERATIONS

Stimming

Some young people may stim when regulating their emotions. Stimming, or self-stimulating behaviours, are repetitive movements such as flapping hands, blinking, tapping or rocking. Stimming isn't solely for emotional regulation – it can also be for fun, due to sensory overwhelm or as sensory-seeking behaviour. In my experience, unless the stimming behaviour is dangerous, you shouldn't stop it. Many autistic individuals stim.

Alexithymia

Derived from the Greek meaning 'no words for emotion', alexithymia refers to the difficulty in identifying and expressing emotions. Some autistic young people have alexithymia, but it's not exclusive to autism.

Sensory links

There's a significant overlap between emotional regulation and sensory processing. I recommend reading Chapter 5 alongside this one to better understand how to support young people who might need extra considerations for sensory input and strategies.

STRATEGIES

Here are some strategies for both school and home to help young people develop their emotional regulation skills. If a student receives support from an external professional, ensure you are also implementing their suggestions of strategies.

IN THE CLASSROOM

These strategies are designed specifically for the classroom, suitable for both teachers and teaching assistants.

- ▶ **Think sensory** – There are lots of overlaps between sensory integration and emotional regulation. So, always have 'sensory' in the back of your mind if a young person is struggling with emotional regulation and see if there are any sensory triggers that could be avoided/removed.

- ▶ **Prepare students for lesson transitions** – Moving between tasks/activities within lessons can be difficult for some young people. Provide reminders and warnings before transitions to help them manage them more effectively.

- ▶ **Check-ins** – Regular check-ins with students who find it difficult to regulate their emotions are vital for understanding how they are feeling and identifying any potential issues early on. These check-ins can be informal chats during breaks or more structured meetings. The key is to create a safe and supportive environment where students feel comfortable expressing their feelings. This regular interaction shows students that their wellbeing is a priority and helps to build a trusting relationship.

- **Extend their emotional vocabulary** – Extend young people's emotional vocabulary by introducing new words that are used to express different emotions.

- **Be caring** – Like many others, I remember in my teacher training being told that when I started teaching in secondary, I must not 'smile until Christmas'. This was because we were told not to show any weakness and be strict until we were more established in the school. Thankfully and hopefully this advice is no longer given out to student teachers (and for the record, I didn't take the advice... anyone who has met me will realise the idea of me not smiling for an hour let alone a whole term would be impossible!). Research has shown that (unsurprisingly!) for young people who are struggling with their emotions, having strong, caring relationships between teachers and students can 'improve student engagement and mitigate emotion regulation' difficulties (De Neve et al., 2023). Therefore, being caring, smiling and empathetic is important.

- **Outdoor learning** – While I fully appreciate this is not often possible, outdoor learning can be hugely beneficial for emotional regulation. So, if there are any opportunities and you're able to take a class outside, I'd thoroughly recommend it.

ACROSS THE SCHOOL

While teachers can use strategies in the classroom to support children with emotional regulation difficulties, having a school-wide approach as well (led by the SENDCo and/or SLT) may enable more consistency. It's also worth noting that many strategies and whole-school approaches are likely to benefit all students and not just those with emotional regulation difficulties.

- **Embed emotional literacy across the curriculum** – Integrating emotional literacy into various subjects, not just PSHE, can help students to develop a deeper understanding of their emotions. For example, discussing characters' feelings in English lessons, exploring historical figures' motivations in history, or addressing ethical dilemmas in science can all contribute to emotional literacy.

- **Sensory space/quiet space** – Just as I advised in the sensory chapter (Chapter 5), having a designated quiet space and/or a sensory area at school for students to use to help feel calm, can be hugely beneficial. Again, be guided by your students and what they feel they need.

- **Thinking from different perspectives** – Encouraging students across school to consider different viewpoints can significantly enhance their empathy and emotional understanding. This can be done through assemblies and any school-wide events. This approach helps to create a more compassionate and inclusive school environment

- **Staff training** – Ongoing professional development for all staff is crucial in supporting and understanding students with emotional regulation difficulties. Providing staff with the necessary skills and knowledge ensures a consistent approach across the school, benefiting all students.

- **Student voice** – Providing students with opportunities to express their thoughts and ideas can empower them and foster a sense of ownership over their school experience. This could be through anonymous suggestion boxes or school councils. Encouraging student voice not only helps to identify issues early on, but also shows students that their opinions are valued.

- **Trusted adult** – One of the most important ways to support a young person in school with emotional regulation difficulties is to make sure they have access, whenever they need it, to a trusted adult. This could be a teacher, teaching assistant, or any staff member they feel comfortable with.

- **Consistent routines** – Changes in routines can be upsetting and challenging for many students. Therefore, I'd strongly advise trying to keep routines across school as consistent as possible to reduce any unnecessary stress.

AT HOME

Young people don't just develop emotional regulation skills at school and therefore the role of the young person's family is paramount. If you're a parent or carer reading this, these strategies might be helpful for supporting your child, but *you* have the expertise on your own child and their needs, so pick and choose which ones will work best. If you're a teacher/SENDCo, these could be strategies you share with the families of the students with emotional regulation difficulties you support.

- **Discuss emotions** – Talk about your own emotions, those you see on TV, and the perspectives of others. Discussing how people feel in different situations and, importantly, how they regulate their emotions, can be helpful. It can be as simple as when you're watching a soap on TV together, stating that someone was upset and discussing with them why they thought they were and if they thought they handled the situation well.

- **Listen** – Perhaps the most important strategy is to actively listen to your child's concerns and feelings.

- **Model strategies for regulating emotions** – Young people learn from the adults around them, so show your child how you manage your own emotions. And be open and honest when we don't always handle our emotions in the best way. Share with them times when you are feeling stressed/worried (within reason so that it doesn't cause extra worry). For example, it could be that if you spill tomato sauce on the carpet, you tell them how frustrated with yourself you are, that you're going to clean it up and then take a couple of minutes to yourself in the other room to have a cup of tea and calm down. Or you tell them when you've had a busy, stressful day at work that you're going to have a bath and watch some TV to relax as a result.

- **Plan for meltdowns** – Have a plan in place that's been designed and planned in collaboration with your child, for when they are feeling overwhelmed. This could include a quiet space for them to go to or activities that help them to calm down.

- **Discuss triggers** – If they feel safe and able to do so, identify and talk together about what triggers their emotional dysregulation. Understanding these triggers can help you both to find ways to avoid or manage them.

- **Try mindfulness activities** – Explore activities that help your young person to focus on the moment, their bodies and their surroundings. Mindfulness activities include intricate colouring activities, breathing exercises and meditation. (Please be mindful that for some children who have experienced trauma, breathing exercises can be triggering.)

- **Explore heavy work** – Any (safe) activity that requires resistance can be classed as 'heavy work'. For example, carrying heavy objects, pushing things or pulling something. This could be helping you to carry the shopping, gardening or laundry! Not only are they often useful life skills, but heavy work activities can be great for some young people to regulate their emotions.

- **Exercise** – Exercise can be great for regulating emotions as well as being a healthy hobby. Try to encourage them to take part in exercises that they enjoy. Gentle exercises such as swimming and yoga are particularly relaxing for some people, whereas others may prefer running and team sports.

- **Journalling** – Writing thoughts, feelings and experiences in a journal/diary allows young people to process the day and express their emotions.
- **Reading** – This is another hobby that can be particularly relaxing for some young people. It can also be helpful to read other people's experiences and emotions and how they deal with them.

STRATEGIES WHEN A YOUNG PERSON IS DYSREGULATED

When trying to help a young person who's feeling dysregulated, either at home or at school, it's important to consider the following. However, as every young person is unique, I would strongly advise coming up with this plan in collaboration with them that best suits their needs and preferences for support:

- **Stay calm** – Keep calm yourself to avoid escalating an already difficult situation.
- **Ensure safety** – Remove any nearby objects that could cause harm. This might mean moving tables, chairs or other items if you're in a classroom or at home.
- **Quiet space** – If the room is too noisy or bright, try to make it quieter and more comfortable for them. Be guided by your understanding of any sensory differences they may have and triggers that could be in their environment.
- **Mind your distance** – Be mindful of how close or far you are standing. Sometimes being too close can be overwhelming.
- **Don't talk too much** – When a young person is dysregulated, it's very unlikely that they will be able to listen to and understand what you are saying.
- **Use visuals** – Similarly, when a young person is dysregulated they may also struggle to communicate verbally. Have pictures they can point to if needed.
- **Recovery time** – They might need a snack, a drink or some time with a trusted adult. Figure out what helps them the most.

RESOURCES

- **Fidget toys** – These are small objects that can help young people who struggle with regulating their emotions by providing a tactile and calming experience. Examples include stress balls, fidget spinners or even just sticky tack.

- **Noise-cancelling headphones/ear defenders** – For young people sensitive to loud environments, noise-cancelling headphones or ear defenders can create a sense of calm. They can also use headphones to listen to soothing music, nature sounds or white noise to help them relax.

- **Zones of Regulation®** – This is a curriculum designed to teach children emotional regulation skills, through the use of coloured 'zones' that categorise their emotions and levels of alertness. It aids children in understanding and managing their feelings by providing them with strategies tailored to each zone.

- **Sensory den** – A sensory den can be either a specially designed space or a homemade set-up, where young people can experience a calming environment through sensory activities. Items like soft lighting, bean bags, weighted blankets and gentle sounds can be included to create a soothing atmosphere.

- **Hydration and snacks** – Keeping hydrated and having snacks available can be beneficial. Sipping water from a bottle or chewing a crunchy snack can offer a sense of calm and focus (if it is safe to do so).

- **Emotion cards and journals** – Using emotion cards or keeping a journal to record feelings can help young people to identify and understand their emotions better.

- **Calm box** – Support them in creating their own toolkit of resources that can go in their 'calm box' to use when they need to. This could be sensory resources or even a chocolate bar and a tea bag to make a cup of tea (if able to do this safely).

FURTHER READING AND SUPPORT

Websites

Zones of Regulation® **www.zonesofregulation.com**

ELSA-Support (Resources for Emotional Literacy Support Assistants) **www.elsa-support.co.uk**

The SCERTS® Model – The Social Communication, Emotional Regulation, Transactional Support model is designed for autistic learners **www.scerts.com**

Beacon House Therapeutic Services and Trauma Team **www.beaconhouse.org.uk**

PANDA approach for supporting someone with PDA as explained by the PDA Society **www.pdasociety.org.uk/what-helps-guides/pda-approaches/panda-as-a-way-in**

Books

All About SEMH: A Practical Guide for Secondary Teachers (All About SEND) by Sarah Johnson

CHAPTER 7
CONCENTRATION AND ORGANISATION SKILLS

CASE STUDY

IEUAN, 14, WHO HAS INATTENTIVE ADHD, EXPLAINS WHAT SECONDARY SCHOOL IS LIKE FOR HIM.

In school, I'm often surprised by how much or how little time I've spent on a task. This affects my work because I either feel like I've accomplished a lot in a short time – only to realise the entire lesson has passed – or I think the lesson is almost over when, in reality, only 15 minutes have gone by. As a result, I sometimes lose interest in tasks sooner than I should and struggle to complete homework and classwork on time. My teachers recognise that I have difficulty managing my time both in and out of lessons, so they often provide extra time for me to complete my work.

Another challenge I face is forgetting my PE kit or equipment for tests and practical lessons. When this happens, I often lose my break times to attend detention or retake the test. Breaks are important to me because having six consecutive lessons without them would feel overwhelming. However, many teachers help by providing the necessary equipment or giving reminders beforehand.

I also struggle with writing longer tasks and essays. I find it difficult to transfer my ideas from my head onto paper, which can negatively impact my grades. In maths, I frequently lose marks for not showing my working out. This happens because I can do calculations quickly in my head but struggle to think through and write out the individual steps. My teachers support me by providing structured paragraph outlines in English, while my maths teacher helps me break down my thought process into clear, logical steps.

Starting a task can be especially difficult, particularly if the lesson subject or content does not interest me. The more interested I am in a subject, the easier it is to engage. Additionally, the bigger the task, the more overwhelmed I feel, which makes it even harder to begin. This often leads to procrastination. I tend to look for distractions, busy myself by helping others, or focus on easier starter tasks because the main work feels too overwhelming. I often find it difficult to recall instructions given verbally and find written instructions easier to follow because they allow me to go through the material at my own pace. Finishing a task can also be challenging, as I find it difficult to return to a task once my attention is broken. Teachers help by breaking tasks into smaller steps or setting consequences for unfinished work, which keeps me on track.

I also get easily distracted by things I enjoy more, such as technology, conversations with friends, or even something as small as a bird flying past the window. My ability to stay focused depends on factors like my seating position, how tired I am and how much I enjoy the lesson. Teachers who recognise my tendency to get distracted often move me to a more suitable seat in the classroom.

Finally, motivation is both my biggest challenge and my biggest asset. When I'm motivated, I can hyperfocus, complete three lessons' worth of work in one session and stay highly engaged in the lesson. I become efficient, creative and proactive, finding the best way to complete tasks properly. However, when I'm demotivated – especially in subjects I don't enjoy – it becomes significantly harder for me to stay focused, start tasks, or complete anything at all.

OVERVIEW OF NEEDS

This chapter delves into two important areas where many young people face challenges: concentration and organisation. These fall under the broader category of 'Executive Functioning Skills' which are essential for task completion. These skills enable us to focus, organise, remember steps in a task and manage time effectively.

While my primary focus is on concentration and organisation, you'll notice significant overlap with other executive functioning skills.

WHAT ARE EXECUTIVE FUNCTIONING SKILLS?

Executive functioning skills are the processes that enable us to plan, focus our attention, control our emotions, remember instructions, organise ourselves and our thoughts and multitask. They also involve inhibitory control (being able to focus, control impulsive behaviour and not get distracted) and cognitive flexibility (being able to think about a few things at once, switch between mental tasks, adapt to how you respond and finish a task and start something new).

Understandably, if a young person has difficulties with executive functioning skills, it can impact on not just their school life but their everyday home life too. Souissi *et al.* (2022) explain that 'Executive functions are predictors of children's and teenagers' behaviour and performance in a variety of contexts, including education, family and social relationships'. For example, they might be late for lessons, appear forgetful with belongings, find it hard to concentrate in lessons, find starting a piece of work challenging, find it difficult to follow step-by-step instructions and struggle to organise their thoughts. Covering all aspects of executive functioning would be too extensive for one chapter, potentially requiring an entire book! Therefore, I encourage further reading if you find young people under your care that require additional support in these areas.

CONCENTRATION

Gazing out of the window during a class, getting distracted by their peers, leaving pieces of work unfinished, not following instructions... As a parent, carer or teacher, it can be frustrating to witness this. While you could argue that everyone at some point in time finds it difficult to concentrate, for some young people, concentration skills are inherently more difficult and there are reasons behind their struggles with concentration.

Concentration essentially means being able to keep focused attention on something. For secondary school students, this could mean focusing on a written assignment in class, reading a few chapters of a book, or concentrating on conversations with friends in the park. Thus, it's crucial not only for academic success but also for building and maintaining friendships.

WHY ARE CONCENTRATION SKILLS SO IMPORTANT?

As young people grow, the ability to concentrate becomes increasingly vital, not just for academic success, but for navigating everyday life. Concentration is a foundation for learning, problem-solving and building independence. For many neurodivergent learners, focusing can be particularly challenging but with the right support and strategies, it's a skill that can be nurtured and strengthened.

Concentration is needed to:

- **Support academic success** – Concentration is key when it comes to listening in lessons, completing homework and revising for exams. When young people can focus their attention, they're more likely to absorb information, stay on task and feel confident in their learning.

- **Develop life skills and independence** – From following instructions to remembering routines, concentration plays a role in daily life. Whether it's brushing teeth before school or packing the right kit for PE, being able to focus helps children to become more independent and responsible.

- **Boost emotional wellbeing** – Struggling to concentrate can lead to frustration, low self-esteem and anxiety. By helping young people to develop focus in a gentle, supportive way, we can reduce stress and create a calmer, more positive learning environment.

- **Improve task completion and time use** – Good concentration helps young people to finish tasks more efficiently and with less overwhelm. This means more time for rest, play and connection, things that are just as important (perhaps even more so!) as academic achievement.

WHO MIGHT NEED MORE SUPPORT WITH CONCENTRATION?

There is a range of SEND that may affect a young person's concentration skills. It's important to emphasise 'may', as all students are unique and cannot and must not be defined by their SEND. Each individual possesses their own strengths and challenges.

Generally speaking, if you have students in your class or your own child with (but not limited to) the specific SEND listed below, they may experience difficulties with concentration skills:

▶ **ADHD** – ADHD can make it challenging for some students to concentrate. There are different types of ADHD: inattentive, impulsive and combined. Not all students with ADHD will face the same concentration difficulties. In fact, some students with ADHD may experience hyperfocus on specific tasks. While the ability to hyperfocus on a task can be incredibly useful for a young person, it can sometimes pose challenges in transitioning from one task to another.

▶ **Sensory processing differences** – Students with sensory processing differences may struggle to focus when their sensory needs are unmet or negatively impacted by sensory input. For example, a student who finds the sensation of a clothing label uncomfortable (or even painful) may understandably find it difficult to concentrate. Read Chapter 5 for further information.

▶ **Dyslexia** – Dyslexia is not just about literacy skills; it can impact various areas, including the ability to concentrate.

▶ **Autism** – Some autistic students may find concentrating on tasks difficult. However, similar to ADHD, they might also have the ability to hyperfocus. It's crucial not to make assumptions based on a particular SEND.

▶ **Dysgraphia** – Often thought of as a 'handwriting problem', dysgraphia actually affects other skills, including concentration.

▶ **Down's syndrome** – Some students with Down's syndrome may find it challenging to concentrate for extended periods.

▶ **Developmental delay** – Since a student's ability to concentrate is linked to their developmental stage, those with developmental delays might find it difficult to concentrate for the same duration as their peers.

An ability to concentrate in lessons isn't just impacted by SEND, but also by whether a young person's basic needs are met. It's disheartening to know that even today, in the spring of 2026, many students across the country are still struggling to have their basic needs fulfilled, exacerbated by the cost of living crisis. As educators, it's important to recognise that there may be students in your class who haven't had breakfast and are hungry, haven't slept well or who live in cold accommodation. These factors significantly impact their ability to concentrate in school.

Before diving into the Strategies section, it's crucial to consider whether their basic needs are being met. If not, the strategies below may not be as effective. Always follow your school's safeguarding procedures if you have any concerns.

OTHER CONSIDERATIONS

- **Sleep** – Have they had a good night's sleep? Adequate sleep is essential for full concentration.

- **Food** – Are they hungry? How long has it been since they last ate? They may have early mornings, long bus journeys, or could be fasting for Ramadan. They might also have dietary restrictions due to a SEND or eating disorder. Also consider the types of foods and drinks they've consumed – sugary foods/energy drinks may provide an initial energy boost but won't sustain concentration levels as effectively as foods that release energy slowly.

- **Water** – Access to water is vital for health and maintaining concentration levels during learning.

- **Trauma, stress and anxiety** – These can all impact on their ability to concentrate. This could range from friendship worries or revision causing stress, to more significant issues such as bullying. Young people may also have anxiety, have experienced trauma or have mental health problems. All of which, understandably, can impact their ability to concentrate.

WHAT YOU MIGHT NOTICE

Students who are finding it difficult to concentrate may present in the following ways in lessons or at home:

- **Difficulty staying focused on a single activity** – You may find they lose focus, find it hard to start a task and/or complete a task. Work may often remain unfinished and they may find revision activities particularly difficult.

- **Easily distracted** – Environmental stimuli such as noise, movement or lights can interrupt their concentration. They may also be distracted more easily by their peers and by screens.

- **Putting off tasks** – They may often delay the start of activities or procrastinate, particularly those that require a lot of focus and concentration.

- **Reluctance toward difficult tasks** – They may demonstrate a lack of enthusiasm or drive for activities that demand prolonged effort and concentration (due to difficulties with concentration).

- **Not following instructions** – This may first appear as them being 'forgetful' or uninterested, but it may be that due to concentration difficulties they are finding it difficult to process and remember what they are supposed to be doing in the lesson, or what instructions they have been given.

- **Difficulty remaining seated during activities** – Students may have a need to fidget, move around, or handle objects while working. At home this might be noticeable during mealtimes or revision.

- **Interrupting others** – They struggle to remain silent when someone else is speaking, sometimes blurting out comments or questions. This might not just be apparent in lessons but also when in conversations with friends and family (potentially causing friendship issues).

- **Challenges with reading comprehension** – They struggle to answer questions about a text right after reading it, possibly due to working memory challenges or because they are focusing on reading the words and, therefore, find it harder to concentrate on the overall content.

STRATEGIES

Here are some strategies for both school and home to support young people with concentration difficulties and help them to further develop these skills.

ACROSS THE SCHOOL

While teachers can use strategies in the classroom to support children with concentration difficulties, having a school-wide approach as well (led by the SENDCo and/or SLT) may enable more consistency. It's also worth noting that many strategies and whole-school approaches are likely to benefit all students and not just those with concentration difficulties.

- **Ethos** – Foster an environment of empathy among students and staff by recognising that concentration and other executive functioning skills can be challenging for some, and should not be mistaken for misbehaviour. Encourage open discussions about these difficulties to promote understanding and reduce stigma.

- **Flexible support** – Consider flexible support options for students who struggle to focus, such as permitting breaks during lessons, providing standing desks, or using fidget tools. Implement quiet workspaces and allow students to use noise-cancelling headphones if needed. Reframe perceptions of concentration difficulties through assemblies, equipping students with strategies to enhance these skills, such as setting themselves goals, developing time management skills and giving themselves breaks during study.

- **Professional development** – Provide ongoing training for staff on concentration skills and other executive functioning skills. Encourage staff to share what's working and enable collaboration on developing effective approaches.

- **Distraction-free revision/study areas and clubs** – Create dedicated study/revision areas in the school that are free from distractions, for students to use during lunchtime or after school. This could be a designated area in the library with minimal visual clutter. An after-school revision club in this space might be particularly useful for students who find it difficult to concentrate at home when revising/studying.

- **Inclusive behaviour policy** – Ensure that the school's behaviour policy is inclusive and supportive of students who struggle with concentration. Review and adapt policies to provide support not sanctions for these students.

- **Less distracting classrooms** – Develop a whole-school policy/guidance on classroom displays and layouts to minimise distractions and promote focus. Encourage teachers to create organised and clutter-free environments. Share examples of classrooms that have been set up in a way that enables focus, highlighting effective strategies such as using neutral colours, minimising clutter and arranging seating to reduce distractions. Remember that many students who struggle to concentrate in lessons may actually be great at focusing but are just focusing on the 'wrong thing' (e.g. displays, projector hum, people outside the window).

▶ **Boost revision skills** – Run revision workshops covering effective revision techniques. Support students to develop their own personalised study plans that work for them and their concentration skills – with breaks included.

IN THE CLASSROOM

▶ **Movement** – Incorporate movement breaks into lessons, where appropriate, to help improve focus. If this isn't suitable and will cause more distractions, try and think of ways to enable certain students to have movement in the lesson that's purposeful – this could be handing the books/equipment out, for example.

▶ **Time management** – Teach students effective time management skills, such as setting achievable goals, creating study plans and using timers (if suitable) to manage their time. There are lots of apps that can be helpful for students to use at home when revising to help manage and organise their study time.

▶ **Repeat don't rephrase** – When we give instructions, if a student asks us what we mean, we often rephrase the instruction to help them understand. While this can be a useful technique, if a young person is finding processing the instruction difficult, then rephrasing is less helpful; instead repeating the instruction in the same way is more beneficial. Encourage students to ask for clarification if needed.

▶ **Seating plan** – Develop seating plans that take into account difficulties with concentration skills, discuss with the student what (if anything) distracts them and where they think it would be helpful to be seated.

▶ **Avoid busy worksheets/presentations** – Use clear worksheets and presentations that don't have excessive information or illustrations that can cause unnecessary distractions.

▶ **Bullet point instructions** – Provide instructions in bullet-point format, or support students to summarise instructions in bullet-point form, to make them easier to follow and understand.

▶ **Highlight key instructions/words** – Use highlighters or bold text to emphasise instructions or key words in worksheets or on the board. Teach students the skill of highlighting these words on worksheets themselves too. This helps students to quickly identify and focus on the most important information.

AT HOME

There are many ways, as families, we can support young people with concentration difficulties. The following examples are divided into strategies for addressing concentration difficulties and methods to practise and develop concentration skills further. A lot of these strategies aren't just helpful for now, but for when they are adults too:

ADDRESSING CONCENTRATION DIFFICULTIES

▶ **Support conversations** – If your young person finds it difficult to wait their turn in conversations and they would like some support with this, you could help them to develop these skills informally and naturally during family mealtimes or on a walk together. Giving them tips on when it's different people's turn to talk, how to know when someone has finished/is finishing what they are saying, etc. Remember to be neurodiversity affirming, only supporting them if they would like help with this and not trying to change them to be 'more neurotypical'.

▶ **Movement** – Encourage them to be active at home and after school, perhaps taking up a sport. Exercise can make it easier to focus. Also respect their need for movement, for example, if you know they find it tricky to sit still at the dinner table – give them the role of setting the table, handing out the meals, etc.

▶ **Breaks during study/revision** – If they struggle to focus on revision/study, suggest regular short breaks timetabled into their revision or study plan. This might be just to listen to some music or do something different, or if they need movement to focus, encourage them to use their breaks to walk around or do some exercises.

▶ **Plan study and revision together** – Help them to organise a realistic plan for revision and study, chunking the tasks, managing the time effectively and scheduling in regular breaks.

▶ **Study space free from distractions** – Enable them to use a space that's free from distractions for study. If this isn't possible at home,

- **Mobile phone plan** – If they have a mobile phone, develop together a realistic and fair plan for how to reduce distractions from their mobile phone during study/revision. This could be keeping it in the kitchen and using it just during breaks, for example. Discover what works for you both.
- **Yoga and mindfulness** – Yoga and mindfulness activities can help young people to focus easier. If they are willing, try out some exercises together or encourage them to have a go themselves/with friends. There are plenty of free videos available on YouTube.

PRACTISE CONCENTRATION SKILLS

- Engaging in enjoyable activities that also allow an opportunity to practise concentration skills can be a fun and effective approach. Here are some activities to consider:
    - jigsaw puzzles
    - card games
    - board games
    - word searches, crosswords or sudoku
    - drawing or colouring
    - building models (e.g. LEGO®)
    - cooking or baking
    - playing musical instruments.

RESOURCES

- **Headphones/ear defenders** – Depending on individual preferences, noise-cancelling headphones or ear defenders can block out distractions. Students can listen to music or white noise, or even enjoy complete silence to help them focus.
- **Apps** – While a little ironic that I'm suggesting their mobile phone can help them to focus, there are lots of different apps available that can be used at home to help young people focus on their study and revision. There are apps with timers, schedules, apps that reward young people when they are focused, and there are even ones families can download that can temporarily stop other apps from distracting teenagers with notifications, all which might be worth exploring.

- **Online mindfulness programmes** – Websites and apps like Headspace offer mindfulness exercises that can be helpful for some young people to concentrate.
- **Sensory resources** – Stress balls, fidget spinners or even just some sticky tack can be helpful for students who need to fidget to concentrate.
- **Wobble cushions** – Ideal for students who need movement to concentrate, these cushions can be placed on chairs to allow for subtle movements.
- **Chair resistance bands** – Attaching resistance bands to the front legs of a chair provides a way for students to push against with their feet. This gentle movement can help maintain focus without disrupting the class.
- **Standing desks** – These desks allow students to stand while working, which naturally encourages movement and can improve concentration. They offer an alternative to traditional seating arrangements.
- **Desk partitions** – For students who are easily distracted, desk partitions can create a more focused workspace. It's important to ensure that students feel comfortable using them and do not feel isolated from their peers.
- **Timers** – Using timers can help students to manage their time effectively and stay on task. It's important to note that while timers work well for some, they may add pressure for others, so it's crucial to personalise this approach.

ORGANISATION

Lost school blazers, missed buses, forgotten homework, misplaced mobile phone... Sound familiar? Many students struggle with organisation skills, but for some, it's inherently more challenging to master. As with concentration skills, it's important to think twice before telling a student off for difficulties related to organisation, as it may be beyond their control.

Working memory skills and organisation go hand in hand. Working memory involves holding information temporarily in your head before using it. Good working memory is crucial for students to organise themselves and instructions effectively. For example, following a set of verbal instructions involves remembering the steps, prioritising them, putting them in order and figuring out what you need to do and how to do it.

WHY ARE ORGANISATIONAL SKILLS IMPORTANT?

As young people grow up, the ability to organise themselves becomes increasingly important. This skill is not only essential for academic success, such as revising for exams and completing assignments, but it also plays a crucial role in developing life skills and managing stress. Being organised can help young people to:

- **Achieve academically** – Effective organisation is key for managing study schedules, keeping track of assignments and preparing thoroughly for exams.

- **Develop life skills** – Organisational skills are crucial for everyday tasks, such as catching a bus on time, cooking meals and managing a budget.

- **Reduce stress and anxiety** – Disorganisation can lead to feelings of being overwhelmed and anxiety. By having a clear plan and structure, young people can manage their time and tasks more effectively, reducing stress and creating a sense of calm and control.

- **Improve time management** – Good organisational skills help young people to prioritise tasks, set goals and allocate their time efficiently. This balance enables them to manage academic responsibilities, extracurricular activities and free time more effectively, setting them up for a positive work-life balance when they are older.

WHO MIGHT NEED MORE SUPPORT WITH ORGANISATION SKILLS?

There is a wide range of SEND that may affect a student's organisational skills. It's important to stress 'may' because each student is unique and not defined by their SEND. They will have their own individual strengths and challenges. Generally speaking, if you have students in your class with (but not limited to) the specific SEND listed below, or if you have a child with one of these SEND, they might experience difficulties with their organisational skills:

- **ADHD** – Many students with ADHD find organisational skills challenging. However, some individuals with ADHD can be very organised and feel more focused when they are organised.
- **Dyslexia** – This diagnosis is not limited to literacy skills; it can impact many areas, including organisational abilities.
- **DCD (dyspraxia)** – Organisational skills can be particularly difficult for some students with DCD.
- **Dysgraphia** – Often thought of as a handwriting issue, dysgraphia can also affects other skills, including organisation.

Other types of SEND that may be linked to difficulties with organisational skills include:

- Down's syndrome
- developmental delay
- sensory processing differences
- autism.

WHAT YOU MIGHT NOTICE

A typical school day for a teenager requires a lot of organisational skills! The routine of getting ready in the morning – brushing teeth, eating breakfast, packing their school bag and catching the bus (or setting off walking on time) – can make the start of the day stressful for those who struggle with organisation. Often, once at school, the need for organisational skills continues throughout the day, with each lesson presenting new challenges.

Our expectations of a student's ability to organise themselves should be mindful of both their chronological and developmental ages. For example, if there is a 13-year-old in your school who, developmentally, is around seven years old, they may not be able to organise their homework and school bag as easily without support.

Secondary students who find organisational skills challenging may struggle with:

- **Starting tasks** – This can sometimes be mistaken for task avoidance, when in fact they just require more support to help them to begin the task in hand.

- **Staying on task** – They may appear distracted or lose focus easily, and require support to keep them on task.
- **Structuring written work** – Organising thoughts and structuring essays or other pieces of longer written work can be particularly difficult without guidance.
- **Finding and deciding on equipment** – Determining what equipment is needed for a task can be challenging, especially so in practical lessons such as D&T and science.
- **Following multi-step instructions** – Remembering and following a series of steps can be challenging.
- **Time management** – Effectively managing their time to complete tasks and meet deadlines can be problematic.
- **Handing in homework on time** – Keeping track of assignments and due dates can be tricky.
- **Keeping bags/lockers organised** – Their locker and school bag may be untidy, and they may need help in remembering to organise it.
- **Remembering extras** – Remembering PE kit, homework, cooking ingredients, etc. can be difficult.
- **Prioritising tasks** – Determining which tasks are most important and urgent is challenging.
- **Self-esteem** – Struggles with organisation can negatively impact their confidence and self-worth. A young person who finds organisation tricky may have low self-esteem as a result.
- **Being punctual** – They may be late for lessons and late for the start of the school day due to organisation difficulties affecting time management. They may regularly miss the school bus or public transport when getting to school.

STRATEGIES

Here are some strategies for supporting young people with organisational difficulties both in school and at home. If a student receives support from an external professional, such as an occupational therapist (OT), make sure to implement their suggested strategies as well.

IN THE CLASSROOM

These strategies are designed specifically for the classroom, suitable for both teachers and teaching assistants.

- **Clear and concise instructions** – Providing instructions in a clear, concise manner makes it much easier for students who find processing and organising instructions tricky. To do this we need to avoid unnecessary wordiness and ensure that instructions are in the correct sequence. It may be helpful to use bullet points to summarise instructions on paper, making it easier for students to understand and retain the information. Visual aids, such as flowcharts or diagrams, can also help to clarify complex instructions.

- **Recording instructions** – For some students, it's beneficial to provide a written or visual summary of instructions after giving them to the whole class. This can be as simple as jotting down key points on a sticky note and placing it on their desk. Another effective approach is to record the instructions verbally on a tablet or device, allowing students to replay them as needed throughout the lesson. This helps students who might need a reminder but may feel hesitant to ask again.

- **Support transitions** – Moving from one task to another or one lesson to another require organisational skills. Support students with reminders and give plenty of warning about upcoming transitions. Visual timers or countdowns can also help students to anticipate and prepare for the next activity (although they aren't suitable for everyone), reducing anxiety and enhancing their ability to manage transitions smoothly.

- **Chunk tasks** – Break down larger tasks into smaller, manageable chunks. Provide a bullet-point summary of tasks to make it more manageable. This approach reduces feeling overwhelmed and allows students to tackle complex tasks more effectively.

- **Visual agenda** – I often feel nervous if I have a work meeting with no set agenda, and worry that I'm not organised; young people can feel the same about lessons. One way you can help is to create a mini-visual agenda/timetable of the lesson using images and symbols to represent different tasks. This can make it easier for students to know what to expect and when, helping them to be more organised and find transitions easier.

- **Organised classroom** – If we are expecting students to be organised, we have to try and model it too! Having an organised classroom with visuals and labels for resources and equipment not only reduces clutter, but also makes it easier for students to find what they need quickly, keeping them on task and organised themselves.

▶ **End-of-lesson routine** – Set aside some time and establish a routine at the end of each lesson for students to get organised. This includes packing away materials, tidying up their workspace and preparing for the next lesson. Consistent routines help students to develop good organisational habits that are really useful life skills. You may find at first they need a lot more time to get organised, but over time this should improve.

▶ **Check-in after setting a task** – After setting a task, check in with students to ensure they understand what is expected. Provide additional support or clarification as needed. Regular check-ins help to address any misunderstandings early on and ensure that students stay on track. For students who struggle with organisation, it's worth asking them how you can help them when you're setting tasks.

ACROSS THE SCHOOL

While teachers can use strategies in the classroom to support children with organisational difficulties, having a school-wide approach as well (led by the SENDCo and/or SLT) may enable more consistency. It's also worth noting that many strategies and whole-school approaches are likely to benefit all students and not just those with organisational difficulties.

▶ **Writing frame** – Teach students how to use writing frames to organise their work. These should be used as a scaffolding technique, and taken away if and when the student no longer needs it.

▶ **Teach time management and organisation skills explicitly** – Teaching these skills as part of assemblies and form time can be helpful. Share tips, advice and examples of how others organise their time and their work.

▶ **Structured routines** – Help young people to be organised by providing them with consistent, structured routines across school.

▶ **Visuals** – Support understanding and access to displays on structures and routines with visuals.

- **Timetable on key ring** – You could print off a small version of their timetable and laminate it for a key ring, helping them to (hopefully) never lose their timetable again!
- **Colour-coded classrooms and timetables and books** – Try supporting organisation skills by coordinating the colours of different subjects, having set colours for each subject and using that colour for the books, classroom signs and on the students' timetables.
- **Communication with family** – Families of young people who find organisation particularly difficult are likely to be spending a lot of time helping their child to stay organised. While it's important to help students to learn how to organise themselves independently without being reliant on adults, we need to get the balance right and offer support when needed. Some students may not yet be at the stage where they can organise their homework, school letters, etc. themselves and need further support to get there. Schools can help by working in partnership with families, passing on important reminders directly to families and keeping communication lines open.

AT HOME

You're the expert of your own child, and you'll know what works for them and what won't work. So please use the following suggestions as just that: suggestions and ideas that you could try if you think they are helpful. A lot of these suggestions will help you and your child to create a toolkit of strategies they can use now and as they get older to help them be organised, and I'd really advise sitting down with your child and making a plan together on what will work for them:

- **Be organised yourself** – It can be really helpful for us to model good organisational skills ourselves for our children to learn. It is also worth explaining to them what you do. This can be in terms of keeping belongings organised, as well as organising work and life admin.
- **Checklist by the front door** – It might be useful to create a checklist for your child to follow each morning, including items like their school bag, lunch, homework and any other essentials. This ensures they leave the house with everything they need.
- **Verbal repetition** – Encourage your child to repeat instructions back to you. This technique of saying instructions out loud can help people to retain instructions easier.

- **Daily homework check** – Make it a habit to check if your child has homework each day. This helps them to stay on top of their assignments and ensures nothing gets forgotten.
- **Time limits for decisions** – Sometimes if we struggle to organise our thoughts, decisions can go round and round in our minds and cause unnecessary worry. One strategy that can sometimes help with this is to set reasonable time limits for making decisions.
- **Use notes/reminders on their phone** – If they have a phone or a tablet, teach your child to use it for setting reminders and taking notes. This can help them to stay organised and to remember important tasks.
- **Organise bag and uniform the night before** – Encourage your child to pack their school bag and get out their uniform the night before. This reduces extra stress in the morning (which isn't a positive way to start the day) and ensures they have everything they need.
- **Desk organiser** – If possible, try using a desk organiser to help your child keep their study area tidy and have easy access to their materials.
- **Triage tasks** – Teach your child to prioritise their tasks by categorising them into urgent, important and less important. This helps them to focus on what needs to be done first and can be a helpful lifelong strategy to reduce overwhelm.
- **Organise homework** – Use a colour-coded folder system for different subjects or types of homework. This can make it easier for your child to find and manage their homework and revision.
- **Organisation apps** – Explore organisation apps with your child that can help them to manage their tasks, schedules and deadlines more effectively.
- **Family planner** – Use a family planner to keep track of everyone's activities and commitments. This helps your child to see the bigger picture and understand how their tasks fit into the family routines. It also helps to set a good example of how to organise multiple tasks and people.
- **To-do lists** – Encourage your child to create daily to-do lists. This helps them to keep track of their tasks. It can also be hugely rewarding ticking off those completed tasks, providing a real sense of short-term accomplishments!

- **Container** – Designate a container for keys, wallets and other essentials. This helps to make sure they are easy to find when your child is heading out.
- **Back-up money** – It can be useful to encourage your child to keep a small amount of back-up money in their pocket for emergencies, in case they lose their phone or wallet. Memorising a parent's phone number is also a useful back-up skill.
- **Bright-coloured phone case** – If they have a phone, some parents/carers suggest having a brightly coloured phone case to make it easier for them to find their phone and less likely to misplace it.

RESOURCES

- **Highlighter pens** – A simple yet incredibly beneficial resource! Students can use them to mark key information in text or highlight key parts of questions, making studying more efficient. Teachers and TAs can also highlight important points in handouts or written feedback to draw students' attention to the essential parts.
- **A watch that vibrates with lesson swap times and hydrate reminder** – This can be really helpful for preparing young people for lesson transitions and also to help them remember when to drink.
- **Task slicing tools** – Visual aids that help to break tasks into smaller, more manageable chunks can be very effective.
- **Clear pencil cases and plastic wallets** – These make it easier to find equipment and their homework in their bag.
- **Voice recording apps** – Using a tablet or phone to record voice note reminders or instructions allows students to replay the information whenever needed. This approach is especially beneficial for those who may require repeated instructions but feel uneasy about asking for clarification in front of others. At home, you might encourage the use of voice note features on phones to create helpful reminders.
- **Voice-to-text apps and word processors** – If a student finds writing difficult, voice-to-text apps or word processors can be a great way to capture their ideas. This allows them to focus on content without being limited by their writing ability.
- **Timers** – Timers can be useful for helping students to manage their time effectively by breaking tasks into timed segments.

However, they do come with a word of warning – it's important to be mindful that some students might find timers stressful and alternatives should be considered for those individuals.

- **Organisational apps** – There are many apps designed to help students stay organised. Simple apps like 'Reminders' and 'Notes' available on most smartphones can be very effective, while more specialised apps offer additional features for task management and scheduling.
- **Task templates/writing frames** – Blank pages can be intimidating for students who struggle with the organisation of their writing. Providing writing frames with sections for headings, images and text can help students to structure their work more easily.
- **Word banks** – Offering a list of keywords for assignments can help students to focus on the task in hand and reduce cognitive load.
- **Specialised computer programmes** – There are various computer programmes designed to help students organise their work. For example, DocsPlus by Crick Software offers excellent templates that assist in organising ideas and tasks effectively.

FURTHER READING AND SUPPORT

Books

ADHD AN A–Z: Figuring it Out Step by Step by Leanne Maskell

Understanding ADHD in Girls and Women edited by Joanne Steer

REFERENCES

Adlof, S.M., & Hogan, T.P. (2018). 'Understanding dyslexia in the context of developmental language disorders'. *Language, Speech, and Hearing Services in Schools*, 49, 762–73. https://doi.org/10.1044/2018_LSHSS-DYSLC-18-0049

Alarcón-Espinoza, M., Samper-Garcia, P., & Anguera, M. T. (2023). 'Systematic observation of emotional regulation in the school classroom: A contribution to the mental health of new generations'. *International Journal of Environmental Research and Public Health*, 20(8), 5595. https://doi.org/10.3390/ijerph20085595

Botting, N., Toseeb, U., Pickles, A., Durkin, K., & Conti-Ramsden, G. (2016). 'Depression and anxiety change from adolescence to adulthood in individuals with and without language impairment'. *PLOS ONE*, 11(7), e0156678. https://doi.org/10.1371/journal.pone.0156678

British Dyslexia Association (n.d.). 'About dyscalculia'. Available at: www.bdadyslexia.org.uk/dyscalculia/how-can-i-identify-dyscalculia

Brugnaro, B. H., Pauletti, M. F., Lima, C. R. G., Verdério, B. N., Fonseca-Angulo, R. I., Romão-Silva, B., Campos, A. C., Rosenbaum, P., & Rocha, N. A. C. F. (2024). 'Relationship between sensory processing patterns and gross motor function of children and adolescents with Down's syndrome and typical development: A cross-sectional study'. *Journal of Intellectual Disability Research*. https://doi.org/10.1111/jir.13118

Bryan, K., Freer, J., & Furlong, C. (2007). 'Language and communication difficulties in juvenile offenders'. *International Journal of Language & Communication Disorders*, 42(5), 505–520. https://doi.org/10.1080/13682820601053977

Carey, E., Devine, A., Hill, F., Dowker, A., McLellan, R., & Szűcs, D. (2019). 'Understanding mathematics anxiety: Investigating the experiences of UK primary and secondary school students'. Centre for Neuroscience in Education, University of Cambridge. https://doi.org/10.17863/CAM.37744

Castles, A., Rastle, K., & Nation, K. (2018). 'Ending the Reading Wars: Reading Acquisition From Novice to Expert'. *Psychological Science in the Public Interest*, 19(1), 5–51. https://doi.org/10.1177/1529100618772271

Chang, Y., Owen, J. P., Desai, S. S., Hill, S. S., Arnett, A. B., Harris, J., Marco, E. J., & Mukherjee, P. (2014). 'Autism and sensory processing disorders: Shared white matter disruption in sensory pathways but divergent connectivity in social-emotional pathways'. *PLOS ONE*, 9(7), e103038. https://doi.org/10.1371/journal.pone.0103038

Chen, J., Justice, L. M., Rhoad-Drogalis, A., Lin, T. J., & Sawyer, B. (2020). 'Social networks of children with developmental language disorder in inclusive preschool programs'. *Child Development*, 91(2), 471–487. https://doi.org/10.1111/cdev.13183

Cleaton, M. A. M., Lorgelly, P. K., & Kirby, A. (2020). 'Developmental coordination disorder in UK children aged 6–18 years: Estimating the cost'. *British Journal of Occupational Therapy*, 83(1), 29–40. https://doi.org/10.1177/0308022619866642

Clegg, J., Stackhouse, J., Finch, K., Murphy, C., & Nicholls, S. (2009). 'Language abilities of secondary age pupils at risk of school exclusion: A preliminary report'. *Child Language Teaching and Therapy*, 25(1), 123–39. https://doi.org/10.1177/0265659008098664

Croll, P. (1995). 'Early linguistic attainment, family background, and performance in 16+ examinations'. *Educational Studies*, 21(1), 13–28.

De Neve, D., Bronstein, M. V., Leroy, A., Truyts, A., & Everaert, J. (2023). 'Emotion regulation in the classroom: A network approach to model relations among emotion regulation difficulties, engagement to learn, and relationships with peers and teachers'. *Journal of Youth and Adolescence*, 52(2), 273–86. https://doi.org/10.1007/s10964-022-01678-2

Department for Business, Innovation and Skills (2012). 'The 2011 Skills for Life Survey: A survey of literacy, numeracy and ICT levels in England'. National Numeracy. Available at: www.nationalnumeracy.org.uk/sites/default/files/documents/skills_for_life_survey/the_2011_skills_for_life_survey_-_december_2012.pdf

Department for Education (DfE) (2025). 'Explore education statistics: Data tables'. Available at: https://explore-education-statistics.service.gov.uk/data-tables/permalink/4d26ec95-b458-41f6-78ec-08dd3ba46a29

Dockrell, J., Lindsay, G., Palikara, O., & Cullen, M. (2007). 'Raising the achievements of children and young people with specific speech and language difficulties and other special educational needs through school, to work and college: DCSF research report RB837.' *Department for Children, Schools and Families (DCSF)*. https://dera.ioe.ac.uk/id/eprint/7860

Education Endowment Foundation (2015). 'Accelerated Reader – First Trial'. Available at: www.educationendowmentfoundation.org.uk/projects-and-evaluation/projects/accelerated-reader

Forrest, C. L., Gibson, J. L., Halligan, S. L., & St Clair, M. C. (2018). 'A longitudinal analysis of early language difficulty and peer problems on later emotional difficulties in adolescence: Evidence from the Millennium Cohort Study'. *Autism & Developmental Language Impairments*, 3. https://doi.org/10.1177/2396941518795392

Ghanizadeh, A. (2011). 'Sensory processing problems in children with ADHD: A systematic review'. *Psychiatry Investigation*, 8(2), 89–94. https://doi.org/10.4306/pi.2011.8.2.89

GL Assessment (2020). 'Read all about it: New study highlights the importance of reading to the whole school curriculum.' Available at: www.gl-assessment.co.uk/press-office/press-releases/new-study-highlights-the-importance-of-reading-to-the-whole-school-curriculum/

Harrowell, I., Hollén, L., Lingam, R., & Emond, A. (2017). 'Mental health outcomes of developmental coordination disorder in late adolescence'. *Developmental Medicine & Child Neurology*, 59(9), 973–79. https://doi.org/10.1111/dmcn.13469

Harrowell, I., Hollén, L., Lingam, R., & Emond, A. (2018). 'The impact of developmental coordination disorder on educational achievement in secondary school'. *Research in Developmental Disabilities*, 72, 13–22. https://doi.org/10.1016/j.ridd.2017.10.014

Hirsch, O., Chavanon, M. L., & Christiansen, H. (2019). 'Emotional dysregulation subgroups in patients with adult Attention-Deficit/Hyperactivity Disorder (ADHD): A cluster analytic approach'. *Scientific Reports*, 9. https://doi.org/10.1038/s41598-019-42018-y

Hollo, A., Wehby, J. H., & Oliver, R. M. (2014). 'Unidentified Language Deficits in Children with Emotional and Behavioral Disorders: A Meta-Analysis'. *Exceptional Children*, 80(2), 169–186. https://doi.org/10.1177/001440291408000203

Khairati, F., Stewart, N., & Zwicker, J. (2023). 'How developmental coordination disorder affects daily life: The adolescent perspective'. *Research in Developmental Disabilities*, 144, 104640. https://doi.org/10.1016/j.ridd.2023.104640

Kuster, S.M., van Weerdenburg, M., Gompel, M. et al. (2018). 'Dyslexie font does not benefit reading in children with or without dyslexia'. *Annals of Dyslexia*, 68, 25–42. https://doi.org/10.1007/s11881-017-0154-6

National Literacy Trust (2024). Changing the Story Evaluation Report. Available at: https://media.hachettelearning.com/medialibraries/hodder/images-and-documents/whitepapers/changing-the-story-evaluation-report-2021-2024-final.pdf

National Literacy Trust (2025a). 'Children and young people's reading in 2025'. Available at: https://literacytrust.org.uk/research-services/research-reports/children-and-young-peoples-reading-in-2025/

National Literacy Trust (2025b). 'Children and young people's writing in 2025'. Available at: https://literacytrust.org.uk/research-services/research-reports/children-and-young-peoples-writing-in-2025/

National Numeracy (2014). 'A new approach to making the UK numerate'. Available at: www.nationalnumeracy.org.uk/sites/default/files/documents/nn124_essentials_numeracyreport_for_web.pdf

National Numeracy (2024). 'National Numeracy Strategy 2025–28'. Available at: www.nationalnumeracy.org.uk/sites/default/files/2024-11/National%20Numeracy%20Strategy%202025-2028.pdf

NHS (2023a). 'Cerebral palsy'. Available at: www.nhs.uk/conditions/cerebral-palsy

NHS (2023b). 'Selective mutism'. Available at: www.nhs.uk/mental-health/conditions/selective-mutism

NHS (2023c). 'Tiredness and fatigue'. Available at: www.nhs.uk/conditions/tiredness-and-fatigue

NICE (2025). 'Attention-deficit hyperactivity disorder: How common is it?'. Available at: https://cks.nice.org.uk/topics/attention-deficit-hyperactivity-disorder/background-information/prevalence/

Norbury, C. F., Gooch, D., Wray, C., Baird, G., Charman, T., Simonoff, E., Vamvakas, G., & Pickles, A. (2016). 'The impact of nonverbal ability on prevalence and clinical presentation of language disorder: Evidence from a population study'. *Journal of Child Psychology and Psychiatry*, 57(11), 1247–57. https://doi.org/10.1111/jcpp.12573

Ofsted (2010). 'The special educational needs and disability review: "A Statement is not Enough"'. Available at: www.gov.uk/government/publications/special-educational-needs-and-disability-review

Ofsted (2011). 'Excellence in English'. Available at: www.gov.uk/government/publications/excellence-in-english

Oracy Education Commission (2024). 'Speaking Volumes'. Available at: https://oracyeducationcommission.co.uk/wp-content/uploads/2024/09/Speaking-Volumes-OEC-v6b.pdf

PBE (2021). 'Paying the price: The cost of very poor adult literacy'. Available at: www.pbe.co.uk/publications/paying-the-price-the-cost-of-very-poor-adult-literacy

Public Health England (2020). 'Best start in speech, language, and communication: Supporting evidence'. Available at: www.gov.uk/government/publications/best-start-in-speech-language-and-communication

Quigley, A., & Coleman, R. (2019). 'Improving Literacy in Secondary Schools: Guidance Report', Education Endowment Foundation. Available at: https://educationendowmentfoundation.org.uk/education-evidence/guidance-reports/literacy-ks3-ks4

Ricketts, J., Dawson, N., Taylor, L., Lervåg, A., & Hulme, C. (2020). 'Reading and oral vocabulary development in early adolescence'. *Scientific Studies of Reading*, 24(5), 380–96. https://doi.org/10.1080/10888438.2019.1689244

Royal College of Speech and Language Therapists (RCSLT) (2019). 'Understanding the links between communication and behaviour'. Available at: www.rcslt.org/wp-content/uploads/media/Project/RCSLT/rcslt-behaviour-a4-factsheet.pdf

Shaw P., Stringaris, A., Nigg, J. and Leibenluft, E. (2014), 'Emotional dysregulation and attention-deficit/hyperactivity disorder'. *American Journal of Psychiatry*, 171, (3), 276–93. https://doi.org/10.1176/appi.ajp.2013.1307096

Snowling, M. J., Bishop, D. V., Stothard, S. E., Chipchase, B., & Kaplan, C. (2006). 'Psychosocial outcomes at 15 years of children with a preschool history of speech-language impairment'. *Journal of Child Psychology and Psychiatry*, 47(8), 759–65. https://doi.org/10.1111/j.1469-7610.2006.01631.x

Souissi, S., Chamari, K., & Bellaj, T. (2022). 'Assessment of executive functions in school-aged children: A narrative review'. *Frontiers in Psychology*, 13. https://doi.org/10.3389/fpsyg.2022.991699

Speech and Language UK (2023). 'Listening to unheard children: Final report'. Available at: https://speechandlanguage.org.uk/wp-content/uploads/2024/03/Listening-to-unheard-children-report-FINAL.pdf

Speech and Language UK (n.d.). 'Educational support for secondary teachers'. Available at: https://speechandlanguage.org.uk/educators-and-professionals/dld-educational-support/for-secondary-teachers/

SpLD Assessment Standards Committee (SASC) (2025). 'Guidance on the assessment of mathematics difficulties and dyscalculia'. Available at: www.sasc.org.uk/news/maths-difficulties-and-dyscalculia-guidance-march-25

STAMMA (n.d.). 'What is stammering?'. Available at: www.stamma.org/about-stammering/what-stammering

Stothard, S. E., Snowling, M. J., Bishop, D. V., Chipchase, B. B., & Kaplan, C. A. (1998). 'Language-impaired preschoolers: A follow-up into adolescence'. *Journal of Speech, Language, and Hearing Research*, 41(2), 407–18. https://doi.org/10.1044/jslhr.4102.407

Tanner, M. A., & Francis, S. E. (2025). 'Protective factors for adverse childhood experiences: The role of emotion regulation and attachment'. *Journal of Child and Family Studies*, 34, 25–40. https://doi.org/10.1007/s10826-024-02989-7

Teacher Tapp (2024). 'SEND: Building for an inclusive future'. Available at: https://teachertapp.com/app/uploads/2024/06/SEND.pdf

TES (2024a). 'Bridget Phillipson announces plans for mainstream schools SEND inclusion'. Available at: www.tes.com/magazine/news/general/bridget-phillipson-announces-plans-for-mainstream-schools-send-inclusion

TES (2024b). 'Lack of teacher training on SEND threatens DfE inclusion plan'. Available at: www.tes.com/magazine/news/general/lack-of-teacher-training-itt-on-send-threatens-dfe-inclusion-plan

The Centre for Social Justice (2014). 'Breakthrough Britain 2015: An overview'. Available at: www.centreforsocialjustice.org.uk/wp-content/uploads/2018/03/csjj2470_bb_2015_web.pdf

The Communication Trust (2015). 'Universally Speaking: The ages and stages of children's communication development from 11–18 years'. Available at: www.fis.cityoflondon.gov.uk/asset-library/tct-univspeak-11-18.pdf

van der Kleij, S. W., Burgess, A. P., Ricketts, J., & Shapiro, L. R. (2023). 'Tracking vocabulary and reading growth in children from lower and higher socioeconomic backgrounds during the transition from primary to secondary education'. *Child Development*, 94. https://doi.org/10.1111/cdev.13862

Wren, Y., Pagnamenta, E., Peters, T. J., Emond, A., Northstone, K., Miller, L. L., & Roulstone, S. (2021). 'Educational outcomes associated with persistent speech disorder'. *International Journal of Language & Communication Disorders*, 56(2), 299–312. https://doi.org/10.1111/1460-6984.12599

INDEX

A

academic success 10–11, 31, 132
Accelerated Reader 46
accessibility 72
  computer 77
  curriculum, for vision impairment children 36
  equipment and classroom/school environment 82
  reading materials 39
  restrooms 103
  water 103, 134
adapted rulers 77
ADHD see Attention Deficit Hyperactivity Disorder (ADHD)
Adverse Childhood Experiences (ACEs) 117
after-school clubs 22, 42, 73, 103, 136
alexithymia 122
anxiety 6, 54, 57, 115–16, 120, 134, 141
apps 47, 61, 139, 147, 148, 149
Attention Deficit Hyperactivity Disorder (ADHD) 29–30, 129–30
  concentration skills difficulties of 133
  emotional dysregulation of 118
  literacy difficulties of 36
  organisational skills difficulties of 142
  with sensory processing differences 91
  with SLCN 9
audiobooks 45, 47
autism 112–14
  concentration skills difficulties of 133
  emotional dysregulation of 117–18, 121
  fine motor skills difficulties of 68
  gross motor skills difficulties of 79
  literacy difficulties of 36
  with sensory processing differences 91
  with SLCN 1–2, 8

B

background noise, reduction of 18, 25
balance boards 85
behaviour impact
  emotional dysregulation 120
  fine motor skills difficulties 69
  gross motor skills difficulties 80
  literacy difficulties 37
  sensory processing differences 95–6
  SLCN 11, 14–15
Blank's Levels of Questioning 26
body sock 110
BSL online free dictionary 28

C

calm box 127
Carey, E. 54
Castles, A. 30
cerebral palsy 67, 79
chair band 110
chair resistance bands 140
Chang, Y. 91
check-ins 122–3, 145
chewable jewellery 110
choice boards 27
chunking 17, 39, 81, 83, 144
classroom acoustics 23, 109
classroom location 102
cognitive flexibility 131
'Coke bottle effect' phenomenon 120
colour code classrooms 23, 146
Colourful Semantics 26–7
communication, definition 5
communication boards 27
comprehension difficulties 36, 38, 135
concentration skills 131–2, 139
  importance of 132
concentration skills difficulties
  of ADHD 133
  of autism 133
  basic needs impacts on 134
  case study 129–30
  classroom, supporting strategies in 137–8
  of Down's syndrome 133
  due to developmental delay 133
  dysgraphia impacts on 133
  of dyslexia 133
  food types impact on 134
  home, supporting strategies at 138–9
  impacts/signs of 134–5
  resources and tools 139–40
  school-wide support strategies 136–7
  sensory processing differences with 133
  sleep impacts on 134
  trauma, stress and anxiety impact on 134
  water impacts on 134
cuisenaire rods 61
Curriculum Framework for Children and Young People with Vision Impairment (CFVI) 36

D

DCD see Developmental Coordination Disorder (DCD)
desk partitions 140
desk screen 110

Developmental Coordination Disorder (DCD) 63–5, 67, 68
　gross motor skills difficulties of 79
　organisational skills difficulties of 142
　with sensory processing differences 91
　with SLCN 9
　social impact 10
Developmental Language Disorder (DLD) 7, 10
dienes blocks 61
digraphs 32
distraction-free classroom 136–7
distraction-free revision/study areas 136, 138–9
DLD see Developmental Language Disorder (DLD)
DocsPlus 27, 45, 149
dominoes 61
doodles 39
Down's syndrome
　concentration skills difficulties of 133
　literacy difficulties of 36
　RLI programme 46
　with sensory processing differences 91–2
dual-control scissors 76
dycem 77
dynamic balance 80
dyscalculia 49–51, 54
dysfluency 6
dysgraphia 68, 133, 142
dyslexia 29–30, 54
　concentration skills difficulties of 133
　emotional dysregulation of 118
　IDL Literacy Software 46
　literacy difficulties of 35
　organisational skills difficulties of 142
　SLCN with 9
dyslexia-friendly fonts 39
Dyslexia Gold 46
dyspraxia see Developmental Coordination Disorder (DCD)

E

ear defenders 110, 127, 139
echolalia 15
emotional literacy 123
emotional meltdown 121, 125
emotional regulation
　co-regulation of emotion 116–17
　definition 116
emotional regulation difficulties/dysregulation
　of ADHD 118
　alexithymia 122
　of autism 117–18
　case study 112–16
　classroom, supporting strategies in 122–3
　due to developmental delays 118
　due to low self-esteem 119
　dyslexia 118
　home, supporting strategies at 124–6
　hunger and 119
　impacts/signs of 119–22
　resources and tools 127
　school-wide support strategies 123–4
　sensory processing and 122
　of SLCN 118
　stimming 121
　tiredness and 119
emotional shutdowns 121
emotional wellbeing 132
emotion cards and journals 127
end-of-lesson routine 145
English as an Additional Language (EAL) 9
equipment 143
　accessibility of 72–3
　breakages of 81
　labelling 19
　lighter 85
　pre-teaching skills of 72
erasers 76
E-readers 47
executive functioning skills 131
exercises 125–6
expressive language 5, 12
extracurricular activities 26, 82

F

fatigue 37–8, 69, 80
fidget toys 127
fine motor skills
　definition 65
　importance of 67
fine motor skills difficulties 67–8
　of autism 68
　of cerebral palsy 67
　classroom, supporting strategies in 71–2
　of DCD 68
　of dysgraphia 68
　home, supporting strategies at 73–5
　impacts/signs of 69–70
　resources and tools 75–8
　school-wide support strategies 72–3
　sensory processing differences with 68
footrest 84
form time 42, 73, 145

G

gaming 44, 70, 77
GDD see global developmental delay (GDD)
geoboards 61
global developmental delay (GDD) 36
graphemes 32

INDEX

graph paper 60
grips 78
gross motor skills 78
  definition 65
  importance of 78
gross motor skills difficulties 79–80
  of autism 79
  of cerebral palsy 79
  classroom, supporting strategies in 81–2
  of DCD 79
  home, supporting strategies at 83–4
  impacts/signs of 80–1
  resources and tools 84–5
  school-wide support strategies 82–3
  sensory processing differences with 79
group work 21

H

hand dryers 101
handles 78
handwriting difficulties 37, 68–9
hearing loss/deafness 9, 36
hearing/sound sense 88, 93, 95, 98, 105–6
heavy work 125
highlighter pens 47, 148
hyperlexia 36
hypersensitivity 89–90, 92–4, 97–108
hyposensitivity 90, 94–5, 97–108

I

idioms 21, 26
IDL Literacy Software 46
inclusive behaviour policy 136
inhibitory control 131
instructions 135, 141
  bullet point 137
  chunking 81, 83
  clarity of 18, 144
  highlighting key 138
  multi-step 143
  recording 144
  repetition of 57, 146
  rephrasing 137
  voice note 19
interlocking cubes 61
interoception 66, 88, 94, 108
Irlen syndrome 35

J

journalling 126
jumbo/chunky pencils 76

K

key word spelling book 41

L

language
  definition 4–5
  disorder and delays 7, 12–13
  processing and acquisition strategies 17–19, 25–6
LeGoff, Daniel 27
LEGO® Therapy 27
Lexia PowerUP® Literacy 45
library, visiting 44–5
life skills 34, 43, 59
  concentration skills role in 132
  fine motor skills role in 74
  numeracy skills difficulties impact on 56
  organisational skills role in 141
literacy skills
  emotional literacy 123
  importance of 33–5
literacy skills difficulties 7
  of ADHD 36
  of autism 36
  case study 29–30
  classroom, supporting strategies in 38–41
  comprehension support strategies 39–40
  of Down's syndrome 36
  due to hearing loss/deafness 36
  due to vision impairment/low vision 36
  of dyslexia 35
  of GDD 36
  home, supporting strategies at 43–5
  of hyperlexia 36
  impacts/signs of 36–8
  interventions and programmes 45–6
  motor skills difficulties impact on 35
  reading support strategies 38–9
  resources and tools 45–8
  school-wide support strategies 41–3
  of SLCN 35, 37
  spelling support strategies 41
  of visual stress/Irlen syndrome 35
  writing support strategies 40–1
long-loop scissors 75–6
lunchtime clubs 22, 42, 73, 103

M

magformers 61
masking 20, 22, 119
maths anxiety 54
mindfulness activities 125, 139
mind maps 19, 39, 40

mnemonics 41
mobile phone plan 139
motor skills 65–6
  fine 65, 67
  gross 65, 78
  sensory input and, link between 66–7
motor skills difficulties
  case study 63–4
  fine see fine motor skills difficulties
  gross see gross motor skills difficulties
  handwriting difficulties due to 35
  literacy skills, impact on 35
movement breaks 81, 137, 138

N

name stamp 78
neurodivergence 20
neurodiversity 20
neurotypical 20
noise-cancelling headphones 127, 139
no pens day 42–3
note-taking 19, 39
now and next boards 27–8
Numberblocks 61
numeracy profile 59
numeracy skills 51–2
  importance of 52–3
numeracy skills difficulties 55
  case study 49–51
  classroom, supporting strategies in 57–8
  complex mathematical concepts, challenges with 55
  cross-curricular challenges 55–6
  dyscalculia 49–51, 54
  dyslexia 54
  home, supporting strategies at 43–5
  impacts/signs of 55–6
  maths anxiety 54
  resources and tools 60–1
  school life and life skills, impacts on 56
  school-wide support strategies 58–9
Numicon shapes 60

O

online mindfulness programmes 140
organisational apps 147, 149
organisational skills 140–1
  importance of 141
organisational skills difficulties 142
  of ADHD 142
  classroom, supporting strategies in 144–5
  of DCD 142
  of dyslexia 142
  home, supporting strategies at 146–8
  impacts/signs of 142–3

  resources and tools 148–9
  school-wide support strategies 145–6
organised classroom 144–5
outdoor learning 123

P

paired writing 40
Pathological Demand Avoidance (PDA) 118
pencil grips 75
pencils 76
pen grips 69, 75
pens 76
phonemes 32
phonics 32
physical models 60
physical needs 100, 108, 134
posture 81–2, 84
practical-based lessons/activities 69–70
praising 57
proprioception 66, 88, 94, 95, 99–100, 108
public speaking, of SLCN students 16
Pukka Pad Vocab Book 28

Q

quiet space 23, 102, 123, 126

R

reading 31, 38, 126
  comprehension 135
  daily reading in free time 43
  fluency difficulties 38
  learning to read to reading to learn, transition from 32–3
  materials accessibility 39
  pens 47
  role models 41, 44
  support strategies for reading difficulties 38–9
  using phonics, teaching 31–2
Reading and Language Intervention for Children with Down's syndrome (RLI) 46
Read&Write 48
Read Write Inc. (RWI) Fresh Start Programme 46
real coins 61
receptive language 5, 13
reminder watch 110
revision skills 137, 138

S

school bell, scrapping 101
school uniform flexibility 101

INDEX

scissors 75–6
seating arrangements 99, 137
Secondary Language Link 27
selective mutism 6
self-advocacy 24
self-esteem 10, 17, 43, 56, 57, 71, 75, 80, 119, 143
SEMH (Social, Emotional and Mental Health) difficulties 8–9
sensory audit 100–2
sensory den 127
sensory inputs 66
sensory overload 96
sensory play 104
sensory processing 88
  and emotional dysregulation 122
sensory processing differences 92
  ADHD with 91
  autism with 91
  behaviour, impact on 95–6
  case study 86–7
  classroom, supporting strategies in 97–100
  with concentration skills difficulties 133
  DCD with 91
  Down's syndrome with 91–2
  home, supporting strategies at 103–8
  hypersensitive 89–90, 92–4, 97–108
  hyposensitive 90, 94–5, 97–108
  impacts/signs of 92–6
  importance of 88–91
  resources and tools 109–10
  school-wide support strategies 100–3
  sensory seeking 90, 95, 97–108
  synaesthesia 96
sensory profile 102–3
sensory room 102
sensory seeking 90, 95, 97–108, 121
sensory socks 110
sensory space 109–10, 123, 140
sentence starters 40–1
sight/vision, sense of 36, 88, 93, 95, 97, 105
silent reading 42
sitting wedge 84
Situational Mutism (SM) 6
SLCN see speech, language and communication needs (SLCN)
smell sense 88, 93, 95, 97–8, 105
Social, Emotional and Mental Health (SEMH) difficulties 8–9
social communication skills 20
  emotional dysregulation 120–1
  neuroaffirmative approach 20–1
  of SLCN students and supporting strategies 7–8, 10, 13–14, 20–1
softer/harder pencils 76
soft furnishings 102
Souissi, S. 131
space hopper 85
speaking frame 17
Specific Language Impairment (SLI) 7
speech
  definition 4
  difficulties 6–7, 12

modelling good speech 16, 25
practice and support strategies 15–17, 24–5
sound disorder and delays 6–7
speech, language and communication needs (SLCN) 3–4, 5–6
  academic success, impact on 10–11
  ADHD with 9
  autism with 1–2, 8
  behaviour, impact on 11, 14–15
  case study 1–2
  classroom, supporting strategies in 15–21
  comorbidity of 8–9
  DCD with 9
  DLD 7
  due to hearing loss/deafness 9
  with dyslexia 9
  EAL with 9
  echolalia 15
  effects of unsupported 10–11
  emotional dysregulation of 118
  home, supporting strategies at 24–6
  illusory recovery of 6
  impacts/signs of 10–15
  interventions and programmes 26–7
  language disorder and delays 7, 12–13
  language processing and acquisition strategies 17–19, 25–6
  literacy difficulties of 35, 37
  mental health impact 10
  primary school, impacts at 7, 14–15
  resources and tools 26–8
  school-wide support strategies 22–4
  SEMH difficulties with 8–9
  SM 6
  social communication difficulties 7–8, 13–14
  social communication supporting strategies 20–1
  social impact 10
  speech practice and support strategies 15–17, 24–5
  speech sound disorder and delays 6–7, 12
  stammer 6
  transient 6
  types of 6–8
  unemployment due to 11
  unidentified 3–4, 9, 14–15
  verbal dyspraxia 7
  visual supports and AAC supports 27–8
  vocabulary difficulties 13
  voice problems 7
speech, language and communication profile 22
speech, language and communication skills, importance of 9–11
speech phobia 6
spelling and grammar check 47–8
spelling games 41
sporting activities 80, 83
spring-loaded scissors 75
squared paper 77
staff/teacher training 42, 83, 124, 136
stammer 6
standing desk 84, 109, 140

sticky notes 47
stimming 121
straps 78
stress 35, 124, 132, 134, 141
student voice 23–4, 43, 83, 124
stuttering 6
synaesthesia 96
Systematic Synthetic Phonics (SSP) 32

T

tabletop scissors 76
Talk for Work programme 27
Talk for Writing approach 46
task slicing tools 148
task templates 149
taste sense 88, 93, 95, 97–8, 105
technology 38–9, 40, 45, 60, 61, 72
temperature 100, 101, 108
text-to-speech apps 47
time management 59, 132, 137, 141, 143, 145
   recovery time for emotional dysregulation 126
   time limitation for decision-making 147
   waiting time for instruction processing 17, 25, 38, 71, 73
timers 140, 144, 148–9
timetables 146
to-do lists 147
touch sense 88, 93, 95, 98–9, 106–7
touch-typing 73
trampolines 85
trauma 117, 134
triangular pencils 76
trigraphs 32
Twinkl Symbols 27

U

unemployment, due to SLCN 11
unwritten rules 21

V

verbal dyspraxia 7
vestibular sense 66, 88, 94–5, 99, 107
video games 77
visual agenda 144

visual aids 144, 148
visuals
   for emotional dysregulation 126
   for literacy skills difficulties 41
   for numeracy skills difficulties 58
   for organisational skills difficulties 144–5
   for SLCN 25, 27–8
visual stress 35
visual task plan 28
visual timetable 28
'vocab learners' school ethos 22, 43
vocabulary 23, 43
   clarification 18
   difficulties 13
   emotional 123
   games 19
   numeracy 58
   pre-teaching 19
   subject-specific 18, 26, 41, 45
   'vocab learners' school ethos 22
voice problems 7
voice recording apps 148
voice-to-text apps 148

W

weighted blanket 109
weighted pen/pencil toppers 76, 109
whole-school audit 22, 42
wobble cushion 84, 109, 140
word banks 149
word games 42
word processor 47, 148
word puzzles 26, 44
Words for All programme 45
working memory 140
writing 33
   comprehension 39–40
   frame 17, 41, 145, 149
   handwriting difficulties 37, 68–9
   paired 40
   slope 76–7, 84
   supporting strategies for writing difficulties 40–1
written work, structuring 41, 143

Z

Zones of Regulation® 127

PRAISE FOR THIS BOOK

'Utterly essential for anyone working in a school. Insightful, practical, and deeply supportive of diverse learner needs.'

Matt Niner, Assistant Principal and SENDCo @wordsfromniner.bsky.social

'An engaging and accessible book packed with practical and manageable strategies to support children with a range of needs. It is a fantastic development tool for new and experienced teachers.'

Sue Issatt, Assistant Headteacher, experienced in delivering staff training

'Packed full of clear guidance and helpful strategies, this book is an essential read for any secondary practitioner looking to develop a more inclusive classroom.'

Natalie Packer, SEND Consultant @NataliePacker

'Supporting SEND in secondary schools brings new complexities for pupils, families and staff alike. This book provides practical, compassionate strategies to create inclusive, thriving environments for young people.'

Faye Whittle, BEP Director of Inclusion

'This book bridges understanding and action with clarity and care. A vital resource for educators seeking meaningful inclusion and strategic impact across all settings.'

Krupa Patel, Director of Innovate Education www.innovateeducation.uk

'*SEND Strategies for the Secondary Years* offers practical, actionable approaches to support students in an inclusive environment. An essential resource for secondary school leaders.'

Dr. Ute Steenkamp, Director of Diversity and Inclusion at Lodge Park Academy